A Lifestyle Of
PRAYER

How To Be A Prayer Fountain

JOE BENJAMIN

Unless otherwise stated, all Scripture quotations are taken from the King James Version (KJV) of the Bible.

Author services by Opulent Books
www.OpulentBooks.net

Copyright © 2024 by Joe Benjamin
Paperback ISBN: 978-1-916691-68-1
Hardback ISBN: 978-1-916691-69-8

www.JoeBenjamin.org

All rights reserved. No part of this book may be reproduced or transmitted in any form or by any means, electronic or mechanical, including photocopying, recording, or by any information storage and retrieval system, without the express written permission of the publisher, except for the use of brief quotations in a book review. Originally published in 2015. Revised and updated edition published in 2024.

Printed in the United Kingdom.

Acknowledgements

To my prayer partner and beautiful wife Josie who is always there to encourage me, the author gives his sincere thanks and love. To our entire team who support us faithfully, thank you guys.

Table of Contents

Chapter 1: Prayer Tanks — 3

Chapter 2: The Three Spheres of Prayer — 17

Chapter 3: A Secret Place — 33

Chapter 4: Fasting — 45

Chapter 5: A Key Ingredient of Revival — 57

Chapter 6: Prayer as a Way of Life — 75

Chapter 7: Praying Nonstop — 91

Chapter 8: Practical Prayer Ideas — 109

Introduction

I have not been commissioned to simply write another book on prayer, there are too many books already. My assignment is to show you how you can make prayer become a way of life.

Once prayer becomes a **lifestyle**, it ceases to be a chore.

Prayer has been made an arduous thing and assigned to the intercessors, the prayer warriors, or the 'spiritual giants'. It should not be so. Prayer is a weapon that has been given to everyone; weak or strong, poor or rich, healthy or sick, etc. All one needs to do is to use it.

Over the years, the lay people have lost their power to pray, as the vicars, priests, and church leaders do it for them. We are living in a season, more than ever, where prayer is not just an accessory but absolutely necessary. One just needs to watch the news or read a newspaper to know that this is true. When you become a prayerful person, you become a partner with Christ. Your prayers will count in binding or releasing things on earth.

Joe Benjamin

Chapter 1

Prayer Tanks

I have been asked to pray for many things in my years of ministry but this was a first. At one of our healing conferences, I was praying for people that had different needs. An elderly lady came up to me with a gentle smile, squeezed my hand and said, "Pastor Joe, I need prayer." I asked her why she wanted prayer and she whispered in my ear, "Every time I try to pray, I find myself falling asleep. I really don't want this because I love to pray". I laid hands on her head and prayed that God may honour her very noble request. She walked away from the front and instantly God started to speak to me. I wish I knew where that lady is now; I would give her this book to share with her some of the things that God told me after she left, which are directly linked to prayer.

It was through moments like this that God began to teach me the deeper importance of maintaining what I now call 'prayer tanks'. These are the reservoirs of spiritual strength that fuel our lives.

There is a time for everything; a time to sleep and a time for spiritual warfare. While Jesus was praying in Gethsemane, He found His disciples fast asleep. He asked them a pertinent question. He could not understand why His disciples could not just pray with Him for just one hour. He was not asking for an all-night prayer meeting or a prayer vigil. He asked for just one hour, but His disciples could not do it as their bodies were weak.

We are living in this technological age where smart phones and tablets have taken over people's lives. A study was conducted and results showed that an average person looks at their mobile phone 100 times a day. What is your daily habit? Does it make you better? Does it bring value to your life and those around you? If your answer is no, you need to change it. I want to present to you a habit that can bring enormous results in your life. PRAYER! Imagine, instead of checking your devices 100 times a day, you pray 100 times a day. Do you think you would be a better person? Absolutely! Your success or failure in life can be determined by your daily routine.

I have looked back in my life when I was at my lowest ebb, when I had my failings and asked myself how it all happened, yet I loved God so much! This is when God started to minister to me about the subject of prayer. He took me to the book of Psalms 51 where David, after sinning against God, went back to God in prayer.

He told me that the reason I failed was because I was not talking to Him and spending enough time with Him. Yes, it was that simple. The more time you spend with God, the less time you have for any mischief.

Think about the story of David. He cried unto God after he had sinned. What if David had the same prayer, supplication, and tears before failing God as he had after asking God to forgive him? Maybe he would have overcome the temptations in his way? This is the importance of prayer. It is like a student who has an examination but goes in with no preparation or revision, hoping to pass. After taking the examination, they start revising; they're already on course for failure. Many times, people pray to God after a problem occurs but fail to take the time to pray before the problem arises.

Prayer Tank

Prayer to a believer is like fuel to a car. In order for cars to function and to be able to drive, they need fuel. Likewise, for a child of God to function they need prayer.

What does fuel do in a vehicle? It provides internal combustion. How does internal combustion work? Put a small amount of high-energy fuel like petrol in a small, enclosed space and ignite it. An incredible amount of energy is released in the form of expanding gas. You can use that energy to propel a car forward. As a Christian, you need internal combustion for your vehicle, called life, to move forward. You need fuel to get your life to where it is supposed to be. If you try to drive a car that does not have any fuel you will not get anywhere!

God has given the believer a fuel called prayer. Many times, you will find people that will go for days without any prayer. And one wonders why their lives are not in order. You will also notice that some people will want to do great feats and exploits of faith with no prayer life to back it up. It will not work.

If ever you want to have any level of success in the supernatural, healing or deliverance ministry, you have to always have your prayer fuel tank topped up. When I am faced with a healing meeting or anything that will need a breakthrough, I will make sure that I have gone to the filling station so that I can top up my prayer life. If you are tired of reading about a God in history pages, but want to see a present tense God in action today, I wrote a book called *'I am Healed'* to encourage you.

This analogy became even more meaningful to me during a particular time with my family as we prepared for a significant event. My family and I usually pray in advance of anything coming our way. For example, we had a case of an application that we were processing that needed approval. We prayed for this situation months in advance until we felt that God had already answered our requests. By the time the actual day of the application arrived, our prayer tank was full. We did not have to pray much then as the tank for that situation was already full. On our family altar, we have a prayer tank for every issue that needs divine intervention.

I am saying that for the different things that you would like to see God do in your life, you need to create 'prayer tanks' for them. If you want healing of a family member, make sure that prayer tank is full; if you would like restoration of a broken relationship, you will need that prayer tank to be full.

If you have to go and perform deliverance ministry on someone, make sure your prayer tank is full. That means you must have prayed enough about the situation so that when you arrive, you are longer praying but commanding it to happen. You cannot start filling your car tank while you are driving on the motorway. This will not work.

There is a story in the Bible about a situation where the disciples of Jesus were unable to cast out a demon. The reason why it did not work was that their prayer fuel tanks were empty. It was like driving a car with no fuel. Look at the verse below and see what Jesus said. This type of situation requires you to pray and fast before you actually start casting the demons out.

> *And when he was come into the house, his disciples asked him privately, Why could not we cast him out? And he said unto them, This kind can come forth by nothing, but by prayer and fasting.*
>
> **(Mark 9:28-29)**

The key here is to pray privately for public results! When you spend time praying in your prayer closet, you won't to need to pray when the time for warfare comes. You simply use your authority as a King. I will talk more about the prayer closet in chapter 3.

When Jesus was in the garden, He knew what was coming ahead: a time of great pain, trial and rejection. What did He do before He went through it all? He made sure that His prayer tank was full. Jesus prayed up before He got to the cross. We saw the same thing before Jesus started His public ministry; He was led into the desert to pray. If Jesus had to pray this much, yet He was the sinless Lamb of God, how much more us?

Prayers are a Materiality

And when he had taken the book, the four beasts and four and twenty elders fell down before the Lamb, having every one of them harps, and golden vials full of odours, which are the prayers of saints.

(Revelation 5:8)

In the book of Revelation, we see how significant prayer is. Every prayer you offer is collected and placed in golden bowls. If prayer can be gathered in one place like this, it means they are tangible – they are substance. You cannot put something in a bowl unless it is coming from somewhere. Revelation also says the prayers (plural), which suggest that there is power in corporate prayer. C H Spurgeon said, "The prayers of a saint are sweet, but the prayers of saints are sweeter!" I believe that this is the time that we need to rise in prayer together as the body of Christ. Never mind your feebleness or inadequacies, because when all these prayers come together, they become a sweet-smelling offering to the Lord.

Prayers are a tangible materiality. Your prayers matter because they are made of matter. It does not matter how small or short your prayers may be – they matter. It does not matter how or where you have done them – they matter. You do not have to feel worthy or qualified to come before the Lord in prayer. In His eyes every prayer matters.

As I am writing this, I see a picture of what this is really like. I see a large pavilion with many clear windows, and a magnificent light shines through – just as bright as the sun, if not brighter. In the exact middle of that room, I see a beautiful table. The material appears wooden and has a wooden feel but it is not wooden. As I walk around this room, it feels really fresh and cool inside. I am feeling really peaceful and I can see through my entire being because of this great light. I start to hear some birds singing melodiously but I cannot see them as they were outside.

As I continue to listen carefully, I hear voices of many people praying, crying, groaning, and interceding. It is like the rushing sound of a waterfall. On that table is a big golden bowl which looks like it has the highest carat of gold. My eyes begin to see what appears to be colourful dried petals of different types of exotic flowers floating gracefully in the air. In a trail, all these colourful petals made their way into this large golden bowl. I see petals for wisteria, roses, lily-of-the-valley, jasmine, lilacs and many more flowers that I do not know. It was a potpourri. My nose instantly perceives the intensely sweet and spicy perfume emanating from this golden bowl, filling the air with its gorgeous fragrance. I didn't want to leave this place because it smelled so wonderful but then the vision fades. This is just a vivid description of how all the prayers of the saints are converted into sweet smelling incense unto the Lord.

From your science you will know about the law of conservation of mass. Einstein is credited to have proved all this theoretically. That law states that, 'Matter cannot be created or destroyed; it can only be changed from one form to another'. The same is true about prayers. God knows our prayers even before we pray; Mathew 6:8. This means our prayers are already there in the spirit realm, just waiting for us to speak and activate them. When we pray, we enter into a partnership with God according to 2 Corinthians 6:1.

Let me take this time to assure you that every prayer that you have ever said has reached the throne of Grace. You may not have seen the result that you expected or you are still waiting for an answer, but that prayer was already converted into something that smells good. Your answer is on the way. I can smell it, the fragrance is very good, just keep believing, holding on and do not stop praying! Prayer has the power to change your situation. If your situation does not change, prayer will change how you perceive and take your situation. Think about it, every time you pray you release a sweet perfume and God smells it. This sweet smell eliminates all odours of doubt and fear. Spray it!

Dear Lord

I pray for my brother or sister reading this book, may their life be one of prayer. May they desire prayer, like the fish need water, like a living creature needs oxygen, like a car needs fuel, like a smelly room needs some good perfume and may their tanks be always full in Jesus' Name.

Amen.

As a shepherd, one of my roles is to be a burden bearer. This means that you often get to hear burdensome news. For example, someone has fallen ill, a marriage is on the rocks, someone has been made redundant, or someone has been involved in an accident. Then I earnestly take these things to God in prayer. I take this seriously as it comes naturally with the vocation to which God has humbly called me.

I was very happy doing this because as far as I was concerned, I was not busy praying for myself. I was standing in for others and was not selfish about my own needs. However, that was the main thing I did whenever I went to God in prayer. There is nothing wrong with this and there is a place for it. However, every mature believer has to get the balance right on what they are praying for and how. The Holy Spirit told me that in selflessly giving most of my prayer time to others all the time, I was missing out on the *third sphere* of prayer. I will explain about these spheres in the next chapter.

Reflection and Application
Chapter 1: Prayer Tanks

---

1. Assess Your Prayer Life: Is your current 'prayer tank' full, half-full, or running low? What practical steps can you take to make filling your prayer tank a consistent part of your daily routine?

_____

_____

_____

_____

2. Minimising Distractions: What common distractions prevent you from prioritising prayer? What is one strategy you can use to minimise these distractions and focus on prayer?

_____

_____

_____

3. Applying Biblical Lessons: How does Jesus' example of praying in the Garden of Gethsemane inspire you to 'pray up' before facing life's challenges? What area in your life needs this kind of prayer preparation right now?

_____

_____

_____

_____

_____

_____

_____

_____

_____

_____

_____

Chapter 2

The Three Spheres of Prayer

There are three levels of prayer that a person can operate within. I like to call them spheres because a sphere represents a realm, a place, or an environment where one can exist. The tabernacle of Moses was divided into three sections or spheres: the Outer Court, the Holy Place, and the Holy of Holies. You can read more about this in Exodus 27. What is interesting is that the word *tabernacle* comes from the Hebrew word *mishkan* which means *dwelling place* of God's glory. The Apostle Paul goes on to tell us that our bodies are that tabernacle today. We should be the dwelling place of God's power.

To enter the Outer Court, one had to pass through the gate. To enter the Holy Place, one had to pass through the door. To enter the Holy of Holies, one had to go beyond the veil. I just want to express this as it symbolises and relates to prayer. The Holy of Holies is the place where only the priesthood, like Aaron, would go and give sacrifices and incense unto the Lord. Then the Outer Court is where everybody else would be gathered in. My hope is that by the end of this chapter, you will be able to shift your level of prayer according to the need. Furthermore, the Lord's Prayer also demonstrates the use of these three levels of prayer.

First Sphere

The First Sphere of prayer is the Outer Court prayer. Most people end here. This is when you go before the Lord and talk about you and your needs. Whether it is spiritual, physical, mental or financial needs, anything that you are needy about, that is the Outer Court prayer. For example, you go before the Lord, and pray for a new job. There's absolutely nothing wrong with that because the Word of the Lord says that He answers prayer and He hears our prayers in Jeremiah 29:12-13. However, if every time you

The Three Spheres of Prayer

go before the Lord you are asking Him for something, you are still at the shallow end of prayer. In the Lord's Prayer example, Jesus passes through the Outer Court on His way into the Holy of Holies (Matthew 6:9) and says "Give us this day our daily bread". It is asking God to do something, to give you rent money, to take care of your personal needs and that is the Outer Court.

As exemplified by the tabernacle of Moses, this sphere was the one that was really crowded. Even today, these types of prayers are what most people focus on. Everybody is asking for something: whether it's cash, cars, or cribs. Yes, God answers these prayers too but there is a more beneficial way of being. Let us move up a level to the second sphere, but before that, here are two biblical examples of Outer Court prayers.

And Jabez called on the God of Israel, saying, Oh that thou wouldest bless me indeed, and enlarge my coast, and that thine hand might be with me, and that thou wouldest keep me from evil, that it may not grieve me! And God granted him that which he requested.

(1 Chronicles 4:10)

For this thing I besought the Lord thrice, that it might depart from me. And he said unto me, My grace is sufficient for thee: for my strength is made perfect in weakness. Most gladly therefore will

I rather glory in my infirmities, that the power of Christ may rest upon me. Therefore I take pleasure in infirmities, in reproaches, in necessities, in persecutions, in distresses for Christ's sake: for when I am weak, then am I strong.

(2 Corinthians 12:8-10)

Second Sphere

While the Outer Court is important, there is a deeper realm that awaits those who seek more. When you get deeper, you get into the Holy Place which is the second sphere. In the Holy Place prayer, you are praying for others. Intercessory prayers fall under this sphere. It is no longer about you; you are stepping out of the picture. Here, you are praying for your brothers, your sisters, the needy, etc. When you go before the Lord in prayer, you say, "Lord, I pray that You help my brother, help my sister, heal them, and bless them". This is a deeper and higher level of prayer. You may find yourself praying to request the gifts of the Spirit to help others. You know, Paul says earnestly seek and covet gifts of the Spirit in 1 Corinthians 12:31. You pray to experience His glory, visitation in dreams and visions, to be used for the good and for the furtherance of the Kingdom. There is nothing wrong with that and there is a need for that in our prayers, but do not

The Three Spheres of Prayer

stop there. Remember my story earlier about how I spent most of my prayer life here? My priorities changed when the Holy Spirit spoke to me.

In the Lord's Prayer, this second sphere is seen in Mathew 6:9 when He said, "Forgive us our debts, as we forgive our debtors". When you start talking about forgiveness, bitterness, and resentment this is already an intercessory prayer because forgiveness is not a one way street. Usually, another party is involved. Here are two biblical examples of Holy Place prayers.

> *And he cried unto the LORD, and said, O LORD my God, hast thou also brought evil upon the widow with whom I sojourn, by slaying her son? And he stretched himself upon the child three times, and cried unto the LORD, and said, O LORD my God, I pray thee, let this child's soul come into him again. And the LORD heard the voice of Elijah; and the soul of the child came into him again, and he revived.*
>
> **(1 Kings 17:20-22)**

> *Peter therefore was kept in prison: but prayer was made without ceasing of the church unto God for him.*
>
> **(Acts 12:5)**

Third Sphere

The third sphere is the deepest level of prayer, which I call the Holy of Holies or the most Holy Place of prayer. In Matthew 9:13, Jesus enters that realm in prayer and says, "For thine is the kingdom, and the power, and the glory, forever". It is a prayer that involves only you and the Lord. It is no longer about you; you step completely out of the picture. It is not about saying, "Lord, give me a gift of healing or the gift of prophecy so I can pray for the sick". That is all thrown out of the window. It is only you and Him. When you look at Him, you do not think about your job situation, your depression, or what is going wrong with you or your family.

In this realm, you glorify God for Who He is and all His magnificent attributes. You will truly see Him as King of Kings sitting upon the throne of righteousness. You see Him as Jehovah Rapha. You do not ask Him for healing as such but you tell Him, "You are Jehovah Rapha and healing is Yours". All you have in your mind, your picture, and in your meditation is just the Lord Almighty. A prayer where it is just you and God alone, seeking more of Him. All you desire is for God to be in you and for you to be in God.

This is a deep realm of prayer that you should strive for.

The Three Spheres of Prayer

Do not put your needs ahead of Him. Do not put others ahead of Him. Jesus is your greatest treasure in the Holy of Holies. Allow that interaction to be an affectionate relationship and a communion with Him. This is the prayer that changes things and moves mountains. This type of prayer requires no effort from you because it is simply you and the Lord, sharing a deep connection. It is intimacy, like how Adam would walk and talk with God in the evening. Sometimes, you might find yourself even praying in the Spirit and breaking into a closed or open vision while you are in this deep realm.

This is the realm that Aaron and the Levites entered when they went into the Most Holy Place to offer incense to the Lord. When they entered, there was a curtain separating them. As the priest went in there, it was a time of being shut in with God in a secret place. There is a lovely song we used to sing:

> *Shut in with God in a secret place*
> *There in the Spirit beholding His face*
> *Gaining new power to run in this race*
> *Oh I love to be shut in with God*

There comes a time in your prayer life where you need to close the veil or the curtain; curtains of what you think or of what people think about you; curtains of what your physical body is going through or mind battles.

Think about Aaron in the Most Holy Place. Aaron would not go in there and say, "Oh Lord, we pray that You provide us with water while we are in this desert". No, not in the Holy of Holies. Upon entering the Holy of Holies, all he would say is, "Holy, holy unto the Lord". Now, this place called the Holy of Holies was a lively and noisy place. Aaron even had bells on his garment as he walked, it was just holy, holy, clink, clink, Jesus You are King. As he walked, even without saying a word, his step was actually saying a prayer. Honour, glorify, bless, and exalt His name here.

Benefits of the Holy of Holies (Third Sphere)

The Holy of Holies is not just a place of prayer; it is a realm of deep intimacy and profound worship where believers can experience the fullness of God's presence. This level of prayer transcends personal petitions and intercessions, focusing entirely on adoration, awe, and a deep connection with God.

1. **Uncommon Peace and Rest**: In this sphere, you experience a peace that surpasses all understanding (Philippians 4:7). The presence of God has a

calming and restorative power that silences anxiety and doubt, allowing you to rest in His sovereignty.

2. **Renewed Strength and Power**: Just as Isaiah proclaimed, "But those who wait on the Lord shall renew their strength" (Isaiah 40:31). Time spent in the Holy of Holies empowers believers. You come out of this place spiritually rejuvenated and ready to face challenges with divine energy.

3. **Revelation and Illumination:** When you dwell in God's presence at this level, you often receive deeper revelations and insights. The Holy Spirit speaks and reveals truths that are not as easily perceived at other levels of prayer (John 16:13). This is where God opens your eyes to His will and imparts wisdom for life's decisions.

4. **Transformation**: In the Holy of Holies, you encounter God in a way that changes you from the inside out. Like Moses, whose face shone after being with God (Exodus 34:29), your time in this sacred space moulds you to reflect more of His character. You begin to embody the qualities of love, patience, and holiness.

5. **Walking in God's Will**: The more time you spend in the Holy of Holies, the more your desires and

prayers align with God's will. Your focus shifts from 'God, give me this' to 'God, let Your will be done'. This deep alignment ensures that your prayers are powerful and effective because they come from a place of pure surrender.

When you reach this level of prayer, expect moments of silence where words cease, and your heart becomes attuned to the voice of God. In this sacred space, worship flows naturally, often leading to spontaneous singing or prayer in the Spirit. You might find yourself in awe-struck wonder, feeling as though time has paused, enveloped in God's profound love and presence.

There may also be times when you are so overwhelmed by His holiness that your prayers shift from words to simple exclamations of 'Holy, holy, holy!' It is here, in the Holy of Holies, that you come to realise that seeking God's face is greater than seeking His hand. You begin to understand the essence of Psalm 27:4: "One thing I ask from the Lord, this only do I seek: that I may dwell in the house of the Lord all the days of my life, to gaze on the beauty of the Lord and to seek Him in His temple".

Earthly Examples

Imagine these three scenarios so we can paint a picture of this concept of the three spheres in order. This is something that would happen between me, an earthly father and my beautiful children.

Scenario one:

Every time my children come to me, they ask me for something. "Dad, can I please have new toys and new shoes?" No problem here, I will give them. Jesus says in Matthew 7:9-11 that we, as earthly fathers, give our children what they ask. How much more the master? We are children of the King and He gives us all we ask according to His will.

Scenario two:

My older daughter comes and says, "Dad, can you please buy my brother a bottle of water because he is thirsty?" I will give it to him and will think greatly of my daughter, who has put a request of her brother instead of her own needs. I may even buy two bottles, one for each even though she did not ask for herself.

Scenario three:

My children come to me and say, "Dad, can we go to the park or the library to spend time with you?" I will take them to the park or library and spend quality time with them. However, I will also feel the need to get them bottles of water and also get them nice toys and shoes. Even though they never asked for the toys and shoes. I am their Dad, I know exactly what they need.

This is the best place for any child to be because they get to spend time and have a good relationship with their Dad, but also get the benefits.

Many times, all we ever do before God is just ask Him for things, when we really do not have Him in His fullness. This is the third sphere, in which I want to encourage you to spend the most of your prayer time. It has added benefits. We should not look at God like a cash machine where you just punch in numbers and money comes out. We need to look at Him as a Heavenly Father who cares for us and protects us, and even knows what we ask before we even pray, as the Scripture articulates.

Be not ye therefore like unto them: for your Father knoweth what things ye have need of, before ye ask him.

(Matthew 6:8)

Do not just be bent on seeking the gifts alone, get the giver and then the gifts will follow. Let me express this with another Scripture below:

Howbeit when he, the Spirit of truth, is come, he will guide you into all truth: for he shall not speak of himself; but whatsoever he shall hear, that shall he speak: and he will shew you things to come.

(John 16:13)

This verse emphasises the point I am making here. The Comforter will lead you into all truth. So, if you are looking for truth, you need to look for the Comforter and truth will be your portion. Do not stay in the Outer Court. Move into the Holy of Holies. I want to show you where that place is. David calls it the *secret place*.

Reflection and Application
Chapter 2: The Three Spheres of Prayer

1. Evaluate Your Prayer Sphere: Based on the three spheres described (Outer Court, Holy Place, and Holy of Holies), where do you currently find yourself most often in your prayer life? What steps can you take to move deeper into the Holy of Holies, where you focus solely on God and His presence?

_____

_____

2. Shift Your Prayer Focus: Reflect on the balance between your prayers for personal needs (Outer Court) and prayers for others (Holy Place). How can you incorporate more time in the Holy of Holies, where your prayers are purely about glorifying God and deepening your relationship with Him?

_____

_____

_____

3. Deepening Intimacy with God: The Holy of Holies is a place of intimate communion with God, free from personal requests or intercessions. What practical changes can you make in your prayer routine to spend more time in this sphere, focusing on worship, adoration, and the acknowledgment of who God is?

_____

_____

_____

_____

_____

_____

_____

_____

_____

_____

Chapter 3

A Secret Place

In my Dad's autobiography called *'My Life Story'*, he writes about my grandmother, Grace and how she had a secret cave for prayer. It was well hidden by bushes and very few people knew about it. In fact, my Dad only got to know about it after my grandmother went to be with the Lord. This was truly a secret place. In the same way that my grandmother had a secret place, I believe every child of God should have a secret place of prayer. Now that secret place does not have to be a cave, up in the mountains or a prayer room, even though this helps enormously. This place should be where you can take yourself away from the cares of the world and concentrate on the Master.

But thou, when thou prayest, enter into thy closet, and when thou hast shut thy door, pray to thy Father which is in secret; and thy Father which seeth in secret shall reward thee openly.

(Matthew 6:6)

In this Scripture, Jesus was giving us the key to a successful prayer. Every Godly spectacle starts from a secret place or closet. He is saying, do not even contemplate praying if you have not yet found that *secret place*. Before God blesses you in front of crowds, He wants to see you in the closet. A place where you can be alone and shut in with Him. A place where you are under the shadow of His protection. Yes, physical locations also help with this. For example, having a dedicated prayer corner or armchair in your house helps your mind to refocus and close out all the clutter and hear God's voice.

The *secret place* is a state of being, a state of prayer where only the Lord matters, where it is only you and Him having communion. This is the prayer that we need to do as a church, as a people. This is the prayer where, when you go into that state, you no longer have to ask God for a job because you are in Shekinah Glory. You need not ask God to heal you because you have already entered into that realm where all things are possible.

As you enter into this third realm of awareness in the Lord, you become very sensitive to His presence. You are so sensitive to the voice of the Spirit that you can hear it. Sometimes, during prayer, God will speak to you and give you a word or a message, prompting you to take your pen and start writing. You do not know what you are writing but the Lord is just flowing straight through you and you are just writing things. After you come out of that anointing and that presence, you read and you think, *Oh right, is this what the Lord was saying to me? Is this how much He loves me?* when you were shut in with God.

Every now and then, you need to find a place and time in your life where you can completely shut yourself in with God. A place where you do not talk to your neighbour, the cat, or the dog. You do not talk to food because you are shut in with God. Food does not even come on your mind because you are shut in with God. You are sensing that sweet smelling aroma of His presence as that incense goes up to His throne. Read Ephesians 5:2, 2 Corinthians 2:15, Exodus 29:18, and Revelation 5:8.

Stillness

We are living in a day where there are too many voices. If you turn on the TV, YouTube, radio there is a voice somewhere saying something. In order for one to hear the voice of God one has to learn the ability to silence all the voices around you to hear God's voice.

I remember once giving someone a prophetic direction to have regular prayer naps. This sounds pretty unorthodox but God revealed that during their time of sleeping they would then be in their quiet place: a place of stillness. Psalms 127:2 says that, "He gives His beloved sleep." That person later testified that during these prayer naps, she found that she was getting many more spiritual dreams than ever before. Rest in the Lord, even when the bills are due, the work deadlines are approaching. If you are resting in the Lord, you will not panic.

Be still, and know that I am God.

(Psalm 46:10)

This beautiful verse above teaches us to be at rest in the Lord. God will not show up on the scene if we are still able and still actively seeking human answers to our problems. When we stand back, He will step up. Prayer allows us the vehicle to do this. When we pray, we are just telling God that we are not able but He is. He should lead us beside the still waters, where our spirit is silenced by His love and grace.

We know from the Bible that Moses was the meekest person on the earth. I believe, as a man of prayer, meekness was the result. Prayer mellows and softens the heart. John the beloved disciple was so mellow he spent time on the bosom of Jesus. Anger issues, pride, low self-esteem, nervousness can all be treated by staying close to God in prayer.

The Lonely Anointing

The eagle anointing is a lonely anointing. Eagles in the Bible represent the visionary and prayer anointing (Isaiah 40:31). "They that wait upon the Lord", also means those people who spend time with Him in prayer. It is in closing your eyes in prayer that your spiritual eyes are open. Eagles fly at high altitudes of about 10,000ft where most birds cannot reach. They are generally solo birds and do not flock. Similarly, prayer can take you to a place that you alone can enter. Prayer is not for flocks of people but for one person, it is personal. Eagles do not flap their wings, they glide on the wind. Believers that have prayer as a **lifestyle** do not flap in fear or frustration; they just glide and rest on the wind of the Holy Spirit.

You cannot hang around people all the time and expect to soar high in the things of God. God is a jealous God and wants to have time with you as much as possible. The people that you hang around determine your attitude and altitude in life. They will build you or break you. If you hang around Jesus, He will fix you.

Jesus had the eagle anointing, which made Him go into the desert alone to spend time with God. In this desert, He was able to be still. This is what you are called to do from time to time. Retreat from people, and relax with God. This involves retreating from social media and social gatherings. Social media is a force for good but can also shape your world and your thinking easily and subliminally.

Whenever I get a bad encounter with some people, like hate mail or negative comments, I start feeling hungry for prayer. This is something that we have been promised. They shall speak badly about us for the sake of Christ's Name. I just pull myself from people and retreat to pray. I go in there like a cat with his tail between his legs and come out like a male lion, shaking his mane graciously. Prayer brings confidence in Christ.

We read in the Bible where David, a man after God's own heart according to 1 Samuel 13:14, would from time to time go into this level of anointing and presence. He is a man who would write songs, verses and sermons that, even up to this day, we can read them and be blessed. He also gives us the secret of how you can enter in, what you should do when you enter in, and what happens when you enter into the presence. He says that anyone who stays in the secret place of the Most High shall abide under the shadow of the Almighty in Psalms 91:1. Now, when you get into that Holy Place, it is like an overshadowing and a covering. It is like a great wind or cloud that is over you.

When you are under a big tree and that big tree has a big shadow, you do not have to wonder where the shadow is because the tree is so big: it covers you. All you need to do is step under the tree, and you know you are covered from the sun. "I will not get any sunburn because I am under the covering of this big tree". Hallelujah! This great big tree is the Holy Spirit. This great big tree is Jesus Christ, Who covers us with His love, grace, compassion, and forgiveness.

So long as you can go under Christ and in Christ, you become a new creature, old things are passed away and you become a new person in Christ Jesus. The old you is dead because Christ has resurrected in you. Is it not good to be dead to yourself, where you do not have to worry about what to think, where to go, what to do? Instead, the new man tells you what to do, where to go and how to do it. Let us learn from David.

Epikaizo

> He that dwelleth in the secret place of the most High
> shall abide under the shadow of the Almighty.

(Psalm 91:1)

In Psalms 91, there is the word *shadow*. If we go to the Biblical Greek, that word is translated *epikaizo*. *Epikaizo* denotes the highest intensity of God's power. It has been used three times in the New Testament: Luke 1:35, Acts 5:15, and Luke 9:34. What David is telling us is, if we can stay in the secret place, we will find ourselves in *epikaizo*. That is where you want to be. The reason why you need to know about this is because this power is available to you through prayer.

We see in the book of Luke chapter 1 verse 35, the story of where Mary met the angel. In verse 35, Mary was asking the angel, "How is it that I am pregnant? I have never seen a man, I have never known anybody". The angel answered and said unto her, "The Holy Ghost shall come upon thee and the power of the Highest shall overshadow thee". That word *overshadow* comes up again, *epikaizo*, this is a peak level of God's presence. This is a special manifestation of the Holy Spirit in your life but you have to be willing to put yourself down.

Parts of the Bible were translated from the Greek and when it was translated, some things were made for the English language. It is important to sometimes refer to the Greek as the English language is limited. If you are a little unclear about something, go back to the Greek and get the meaning of it. I am an avid Greek student for this same reason.

If you break that word *epikaizo* - *epi* and *kaizo* are two separate words put together. *Epi* means to block or cover over something and *kaizo* means shadow. So, before you get into this presence, as you pray, make sure everything is blocked out. Block your own mind, your own thinking, and your own doubts. It is time you need to doubt your doubts. Why is it that we believe our doubts more than we believe the word of God? We believe what the doctor says more than we believe the word of God. You believe what your enemies say more than you believe the word of God.

When the Holy Ghost came upon the apostles in Acts 5, it was an overshadowing. These people had been praying in the Upper Room and waiting upon the Lord for days. They had gone past the level one of prayer, where they probably prayed: "Lord we pray that Your Word may come to pass"; they had gone past that level. They had gone past praying: "Lord we want to see those things that Jesus spoke about".

They had stopped praying about their unsaved families. They were on the third sphere of prayer, where they were just waiting upon the Lord.

I can see them sing....

> *We wait for you*
> *We wait for you*
> *We wait for you*
> *To walk in the room*

It is when you get to that level that you really start to appreciate God's grace. Your life is laid bare before you. All that beating up your chest saying 'I am the man', 'I know it all', 'I am clever', 'I have been saved for 30 years', 'I have prayed for people', 'I have brought people to Christ'; all that becomes nothing before the Lord. You just look at yourself and say, "Lord, what a wretched sinner I am". That is when His grace takes over. That is when His forgiveness and His love for you takes over and as you pray, focus on the Master. Do not focus on yourself and life will be so much easier.

Commit today to finding your secret place, where you can be enveloped by His presence and experience the fullness of His glory.

Reflection and Application
Chapter 3: A Secret Place

---

1. Identify Your Secret Place: Do you have a dedicated secret place for prayer where you can be alone with God? If not, what physical or mental space can you create to develop this sacred time of uninterrupted communion with the Lord?

_____

_____

_____

2. Practicing Stillness: In a world filled with constant noise and distractions, how can you intentionally practice stillness to hear God's voice more clearly? What steps can you take to silence the external and internal voices that compete for your attention during prayer?

_____

_____

_____

3. Understanding Epikaizo: The chapter mentions the concept of *epikaizo*, or the highest intensity of God's power. How can you position yourself spiritually to experience this overshadowing presence of God in your prayer life? Reflect on the areas of your life where you need to block out distractions and fully surrender to His will.

_____

_____

_____

_____

_____

_____

_____

_____

_____

_____

Chapter 4

Fasting

I remember in 2003 when I was living in Sheffield and God put me on a fast. I did not plan it, neither did I desire it. It was an impression from God and He took my appetite away for three days. Deep down in my spirit I knew what was troubling me. I had been on the run and avoiding the call of God on my life. My dad is a preacher and many people expected me, as the first son, to just be like him. The rebel in me wanted to just pursue other avenues in life. If I had not obeyed the fast, I would have not even had the experience I had.

During my time of fasting, I found myself praying and confessing my weakness and inadequacies to the Lord. I came up with every excuse under the sun. I was saying, "Lord, I am not capable of carrying the torch of your Word." I just wanted to have an easy and free life. I had seen ministry firsthand as a pastor's child – it is not a joy ride. I was trying to negotiate my way out of it. However, the burden of the call did not leave me; it kept pressing on me. Even by the second day of fasting, when I didn't feel hungry, I was growing desperate. I felt as though if I went against what God was imprinting on my heart, I would die. I think of Jesus in the garden praying, 'Father, let this cup pass'. The cup did not pass because it was His cup. Whatever cup He gives you, drink it!

On Sunday, I went to church still feeling heavy, carrying the weight of what God was impressing on my heart. I needed an answer. I prayed and said, "Lord, you need to speak or I will be a dead man". I lost the tug of war. The whole service I was lying prostrate on the altar area. I was weak and had resolved before the Lord that I was not going to get up until I had been excused from the call. As I was groaning in the spirit, my spirit was praying and then I heard my spirit saying, "Lord, whatever you want me to do to serve you, I will do it."

At that point, a heavy load was released from my being. I felt lighter. I felt strength coming into my body. I felt a meek smile creep upon my face. I had just accepted God's call for ministry on my life. As I stood up as the last person to leave the church, I met a lady outside who remarked that my face was glowing. It was interesting to know that my face was glowing even though I had been on a three-day and hadn't told anyone about it. Jesus in Mathew 6:16 said that, "When you go on a fast you must not look miserable in order for you to get praise from people." This is simply because if people praise you, there is little room left for God to bless you. Human acclaim can also breed pride; therefore, to remain humble, it is wise to fast discreetly. This will allow God Himself to bless you in a way that no human praise can do.

I am reminded of Moses when he went into God's presence for forty days on Mount Sinai. When he came back down his face was glowing and radiating God's presence. I was not aware of it but it was the Glory of God and it was confirmation that I had been in His presence. I am telling you this story because it happened when I was on a fast. I am not saying that every time you fast you will see God, neither am I saying if you do not fast you cannot meet God. All I am saying is, if God calls you to fast, obey. He has something in store for you. When you are on a fast, you are focused and your spirit is in tune with Gods voice and your expectation is high.

I usually fast at least once a week and I think it is reasonable for an able believer to do that. Whenever I fast, I am reminded of the Holy Spirit's nearness to me, and my antenna for downloading from Him is sharp. I do not do it as a law; I do it as a lifestyle of grace. It is a routine that has become a part of my Christian life. God has done so much for me, and I love to just be with Him as much as I can.

Fasting in the Bible

A fast is a conscious deliberate decision to abstain for a time from the pleasure of eating in order to gain important spiritual benefits. Fasting is mentioned in Scripture one-third as often as prayer. This suggests to us that you cannot effectively live **a lifestyle of prayer** if you do not live a lifestyle of fasting. These two work hand in hand. Fasting is biblical and we know that great men of God like Moses, David, Paul and even Jesus fasted.

There are many types of fasts that an individual can do:

Total/Absolute fast – You don't drink any water or eat any food. In the Bible, we have an example of this in Esther 4:15-16. Here, Esther declared a three day's fast with no water or food.

Water fast – This is when you drink water only throughout the fast. In Matthew 4:2, Jesus went for a fast and afterwards, the Bible says He was hungry. It however does not mention that He was thirsty. Does this suggest Jesus was on a water fast?

Partial fast – This is a readjustment of your diet or eating regime. It could be that you eat fruits only, juice, limited meals per day, etc. There is an example on this fast in Daniel 10:2-3. Here, Daniel only ate vegetables and water, no meat or wine.

It has to be mentioned that before you embark on a fast, you need to check that you are fit and well to do so. You may need to check with your doctor.

The other fasts that people can do, which does not involve eating or drinking are fasting from Television, social media, negative thoughts, etc. Anything that can take your time away from time with God can be fasted from. Similarly, when you fast from food, your goal should be to at least match the time you've saved by spending it with God. For example, using your one-hour lunch break to spend an hour with God. Remember, fasting is not just about abstaining from food but a means of deepening the relationship with God. Without prayer and seeking His presence, a fast becomes nothing more than a hunger strike.

Prayer and fasting work together like Siamese twins. If you fast but never spend the time with God, you will miss out on the full benefits of fasting, which I want to share with you now.

The Fasted Life

I live on this principle. The fasted life is not about viewing fasting as a one-off event or an occasional spiritual exercise. It is a **lifestyle**: a continuous walk with God where fasting becomes a natural part of your spiritual journey. Imagine dedicating one day each week to fasting, skipping a meal occasionally, or choosing to abstain from certain types of food on the go. These practices, when done with the right heart, help you remain spiritually aligned and in tune with God's will.

Fasting is not about following a rigid law or trying to gain God's approval through works. We don't fast because we must; we fast because we want to respond to God's abundant grace. Fasting under grace is a joyful act of devotion, not a burden. As believers, we are called to fast not out of competition but as a way to draw closer to God and experience His power in our lives.

The Benefits of Fasting

When you fast, you are disciplining your body. What this means is that you're telling your body to be aware that the spirit man is in charge. Many times, we are led by how our bodies feel and our feelings are not always accurate. Feelings are nothing more than emotions which can be created and can also be dismantled. We should only be moved by the Word of God. Imagine if your spirit man was always in control, you would be very alert and sensitive to God's presence and direction.

Fasting shows your humility to God. You should not fast because you have to. You fast because you love Him and you want to be closer to Him. You cannot fast so that you are seen to be good, or to punish yourself from your sins. Remember, God's grace is bigger than what you can ever do. You are saved by Grace, and nothing you do – good or bad – will make Him love you any more or less.

I have found fasting to be an efficient propeller to my prayers. In 1 Samuel 1:7, we learn about a woman called Hannah who was fasting and praying for a son. I believe that the fasting helped propel the answer to her request. This is like a boat with a motor engine propeller. If the boat is on the water with no propeller, it will sail and stay afloat. This is the level where prayer is just done as usual.

However, when fasting and prayer are combined, it's like turning on the engine of the boat. This propels the boat more easily, helping the sailor reach the destination faster with less resistance. This is the power of fasting. Whenever you come across a situation in your life that is difficult and you see no changes, try to fast specifically for that situation. It works because your faith is raised, your sincerity levels are up, and you are at a humble place.

The Bible teaches us to fast and pray. When we do it, we are simply obeying God's Word. It does not make us righteous or any better than anyone else. Obedience always releases the blessings that are attached to the instruction. In our quest for righteousness and holiness, fasting is a torch on our path. There is a definite blessing that comes from fasting. Jesus said, *Blessed are those that will hunger and thirst for righteousness.*

One of the marginal, yet extra benefits of fasting, is divine health. Divine health is the state of being free from illness or injury because of living according to God's plan and within His will. This is because science has proven that fasting helps detoxify the body. Well, a spiritual detoxification is also done concurrently.

There is a difference between Divine healing and Divine health. Divine healing is divine intervention which resolves a physical, emotional or spiritual problem. Many times, all we want is Divine healing. However, if you stay healthy in line with God's laws, you won't need healing, as you will already be healthy. Here is what I mean.

God has put natural laws on the earth. (Genesis 1:1, Psalm 24:1) For example if you stand on top of that high roof and you jump off, you might fall down and might break an arm. If you fall off that roof, it is because of the law of gravity. This is a law that God has already set before the foundation of the world.

If you drink too much alcohol, you may have liver cirrhosis. If you do not look at what you eat, and you just eat anything, what happens? You could become obese and would then become a high risk for type two diabetes. If you eat too much sugar, you will have caries (tooth decay). If you smoke, you are at a higher risk of developing cancer. In order for us to have Divine Health, we need to abide by God's laws over our lives.

Reflection and Application
Chapter 4: Fasting

---

1. Reflecting on Your Motivation: What has been your primary motivation for fasting in the past? How can you align your future fasting practices to reflect genuine humility and a sincere desire to draw closer to God?

_____

_____

_____

2. Evaluating Your Fasting Routine: How often do you currently fast, and how does it impact your spiritual life? What steps can you take to incorporate regular fasting into your **lifestyle** as a way to strengthen your relationship with God and maintain spiritual sensitivity?

_____

_____

_____

3. Applying Fasting for Breakthroughs: Reflect on a specific challenge or situation in your life that has remained unchanged despite your prayers. How can you apply the principles of fasting shared in this chapter to seek God's guidance and breakthrough in this area?

_____

_____

_____

_____

_____

_____

_____

_____

_____

_____

_____

Chapter 5

A Key Ingredient of Revival

Leonard Ravenhill once said, "We've said that prayer changes things. No! Prayer does not change things. Prayer changes people and they change things. There's nothing more transfiguring than prayer." I feel that this quote is on point and the reason why I say so is, if we can pray enough until we are changed, we become the revival. Do not pray and say Lord send a revival, pray and say Lord make me the revival. You are the revival! The power of the Holy Spirit in you makes you a powerhouse. It makes you stronger than an atomic bomb when you get on your knees.

Fires Vision

Just before we relocated to Somerset, I saw a vision of a fire that had ignited in a place. As the vision unfolded, I saw the fire catch on in another place nearby, then another and another. This happened at lightning speed until all the fires converged together into one big bonfire. As the bonfire grew and increased in intensity, there was a queue of people coming around to watch it burn. Scores of people gathered around the fire and many more kept coming. The fire continued on for many days and the people were not abated. A famous speaker once said, "Put yourself on fire for God and the world will come and watch you burn". I believe the time is ripe for another large Holy Spirit fire to engulf the body of Christ.

The Revival Triangle

Science tells us that in an earthly fire, there are three things that make up the combustion triangle. Fuel, heat, and oxygen. In my illustration of a supernatural fire being the revival, I propose that the three main ingredients of a spiritual revival are as follows:

- Fuel is prayer.
- Heat is the undiluted Word of God.
- Oxygen is the Holy Spirit.

A Key Ingredient of Revival

Take a close look at this verse below, clearly explaining how important prayer is in the spiritual revival triangle.

God says, if My people PRAY and seek My face, I will hear from heaven and bring revival.

> *If my people, which are called by my name, shall humble themselves, and pray, and seek my face, and turn from their wicked ways; then will I hear from heaven, and will forgive their sin, and will heal their land.*
>
> **(2 Chronicles 7:14)**

The same verse tells us that to experience revival, we must to turn from our wicked ways by obeying the precepts of the Word of God. James also says that we have to clean our hands from the ungodly things and things that are not pleasing to the Father. See what James says below:

> *Draw nigh to God, and he will draw nigh to you. Cleanse your hands, ye sinners; and purify your hearts, ye double minded.*
>
> **(James 4:8)**

In the Old Testament, the priest had to cleanse his entire body with water before going into the Holy of Holies. In the New Testament, we no longer have to wash with actual water. The water is the Word of God which makes us clean spiritually.

The Holy Spirit is a necessary component. If you need to check that fact, ask the guys in the Upper Room. They waited and prayed but until the Holy Spirit came, there was no revival. In the book of Acts 2 the Bible says, "Suddenly there came a sound from heaven as of a rushing mighty wind, and it filled the entire house where they were sitting". This is the wind that will keep any revival fire burning. I am troubled when I see people and churches that have rejected the Holy Spirit to operate and move among them. The Holy Spirit is not a fairy tale; it is a living reality and a touchable materiality.

If anything in this combustion triangle is removed, the revival fires die. We cannot control spiritual revival like we do natural fires. God sends revivals and sustains them. However, we will not get any revival until our hearts and hands are ready to receive it. It is like the Parable of The Sower, where there had to be good ground for good results to come forth. Our prayer and goal are to ensure our vessels are prepared.

Prayer is something that is within our reach, power, and permission. It is something that we have been given as a tool to bring heaven on earth. James 5:16 says that the effectual, fervent prayer of a righteous man is powerful and effective. I see a generation of believers rising up that will use that power to keep the church revived and alive. If you examine a common trend in all past revivals, you'll notice that as long as the people kept praying, the revival continued. However, when they shifted their focus from prayer to programs and projects, the fire gradually began to fade until there was no heat left at all.

It ends up as a dead, powerless religion. I know that every revival had vital lessons that we can learn from, but this is not the place or time to critique. I just want to share with you how prayer affected a few past revivals. Other debates and discussions on the rights and wrongs can be done on another day.

Aimee Semple McPherson

Aimee Semple McPherson (1890 - 1944) was the founder of the Foursquare church. After she was born again, she started to look for more of God. She started to attend prayer meetings where people were 'tarrying' on the Holy Ghost. She would even skip school to attend prayer meetings. It is from this background that her healing ministry started. Prayer was key.

Brownsville Revival

This revival was spearheaded by the late evangelist Steve Hill from 1995 to about 2000. The church in Pensacola Florida, USA saw about four million people walk through their doors. I remember watching this revival on gospel television and all I remember is people coming to the altar, tears streaming down their cheeks and praying. The main message was repentance and a strong call to prayer. By just watching Steve minister, you wouldn't need anyone to tell you that he was a man of prayer. Many times, he would minister with tears streaming down his cheeks. He used to have regular altar calls for sinners. The church has forgotten what an altar call looks like. May God help us!

The Welsh Revival

In 1904, God raised a man called Evan Roberts, a coal miner in South Wales. He was only 26 when the revival broke out. This was a great revival that struck the United Kingdom. History reports that, within a space of about two years, over one hundred thousand people were saved. He was a great man of prayer. The revival was birthed from the womb of prayer. The question is, we all love revival but are we prepared to pay the price for a true awakening?

A Key Ingredient of Revival

Roberts would seek the Lord in the middle of the night until his bed shook. He would be awakened by the Lord at 1am and he would pray for hours. This happened to him nightly for three months before the revival started. Crime rates in Wales went down, the pubs went empty, and policemen spent their time at the revival meetings. Services were done every day, instead of just on Sundays. God was on the move.

During the revival, a bunch of theological dignitaries from the USA went to Wales to see the revival. When they arrived, they saw a policeman who was walking about happily waving his police baton and singing *Down at the Cross where my Saviour died.* They stopped him and asked if he knew where the Welsh Revival was. The policeman looked to him and said, "You have arrived! The revival is here, I am the revival". What a lesson. Many times, we want to assign revival to a place or situation, but actually true revival is us. When you become the revival, you can help ignite others to also get revived. We know that the Welsh Revival spread far and wide, even across the borders to other countries.

The Moody Revival

American Dwight L. Moody, born in 1837, was used by God as an instrument for revival. He was uneducated but this means nothing before God. Many people that God has used in the past, even in the Bible, have been people that were not highly educated. You do not need education to be used by God. You need **a lifestyle of prayer**. Moody was saved as a result of someone's prayers over his life. Can you see how powerful prayer is? Keep on praying, it was this prayer that helped bring a man on the scene that was an instrument of revival.

D. L. Moody was a man that was committed to prayer and fasting. Many nights of prayer and waiting on the Lord was a lifestyle. One time, D. L. Moody needed twenty thousand dollars to pay off some ministry needs. He did not ask anyone for that money, but told his friend that he was going to get that money by prayer! God provided it in a miraculous way. Many times, we tell people about our financial problems, yet those people cannot help us, they also need a loan! Ask God, He owns the silver and gold.

Moody was a great revivalist and preacher. What made him a great preacher was **a lifestyle of prayer**. In his words, "If we want a revival in our churches, we must pray for it. It isn't great preaching that we want, brethren, so much as it is great praying". Dear preachers and ministry servants who help in the vineyard of the Lord, if you want to be great in the kingdom, prayer is the key. If you lead worship or preach, you cannot lead people to a place that you have never been. If you can get into this place of prayer at home alone before you come in front of the people, you will be effective as people can sense and feel that you are coming from a place of prayer, not just duty or routine. It is Mr Moody who once said: "He who kneels the most, stands the best". Profound!

Voice of Healing Revival

When I was living in London, for three years I had a quotation that I stuck up on my fridge door by W. M. Branham. It read: "If you'll put your face in God's Word, and your eyes towards Heaven, and let your pants' legs be bagged at the knees, be reverent before God, there'll be someday that God will take you over to one side, and give to you a power and a gift that the whole world will know He's been with you". What an inspirational quote on prayer!

William M. Branham was born in USA in 1909. He is considered by many to be the initiator of healing and charismatic revival that began in 1947. Rev. Branham circled the globe seven times, holding some of the largest meetings in history. In the book called *A Prophet visits South Africa* by Julius Stadsklev, there are details about the mighty works wrought through this man by God. Some 100,000 people heard him in Durban, South Africa. Seven truckloads of crutches, wheelchairs, canes, etc., were hauled away after the healing services.

This revival and vessel were born from a life of prayer. He would frequent the mountains and a cave to pray. It was when he was that praying amazing things would happen. For example, one day, while praying with his hands lifted up, a supernatural sword was placed in his hand. On many occasions during prayer and fasting, he received precise visions of healings that were about to occur. To whom much is given much is required. If God has given you some spiritual gifts or talents, you need to sharpen and purify them by prayer.

John Knox

Scottish reformer John Knox's name became synonymous with prayer. He is known for his famous plea: *'Lord, give me Scotland, or I die!'* And God granted his request. Starting in 1559, he travelled far and wide, preaching reformation. Let us pause for a minute of reflection. John was so burdened for Scotland to be saved that his life did not mean much to him. Many times, we still love our sausages, egg, and beans so much that it becomes a priority in life, instead of the spiritual things.

How desperately do you want to see people saved and healed? Who is prepared to stand in the gap and intercede for this dying nation and world? Who is prepared to miss a meal or two? Who is ready to say 'my life means nothing unless God comes down'? This was the kind of man that Knox was.

My dad once purposed in his heart to the Lord and said, "Lord, if You do not send revival to our church, You will find a pile of bones on this altar". Think about it for a minute. That sincere and honest prayer hit the Throne and revival broke out in his church.

Charles G. Finney Revival

If you are a student of past revivals like me, you will know Charles Finney (1792 - 1875). He is considered one of the giants of American revivalism. Charles was a great preacher, revivalist and a qualified lawyer. If you have read about Finney, you will have come across a significant man in his ministry called Daniel Nash (1775 - 1831). It is Minister Nash, the prayer warrior, I want to highlight here. He

A Lifestyle of Prayer

was a man of prayer and committed to intercession. His role as an intercessor initially came about when he was ill and had lost his sight. All he spent his time doing then was praying. Later on, God healed him, but he remained an intercessor. He met with Finney and they would travel the country together.

Nash was notorious for prayer. What a reputation! Would it not be wonderful for you to be known as a person of prayer? Rather than to be known as a gossiper, liar or cheat? Nash prayed so much that it is said you could hear him praying half a mile away. Father Nash committed his life to praying for revival and interceding for the ministry of Charles Finney. Whenever Finney had a revival meeting, Father Nash would get into that city before him to find a lodging, gather a few willing intercessors and pray for the meetings. It is said many times that he would not even attend the services, as he was fasting and praying for Charles throughout the meetings. God just showered a great grace on his life and no one can do this unless the Father calls you into it and equips you. This is not limited to a select few; as long as you are willing to be used by God, He is able.

God will call some people and put them in the fore front like pastors and leaders. He will also call others and place them in the background as support structure to pray for their leader. This is a rare anointing, especially nowadays where everyone wants to have the microphone and take centre stage. However, if God calls you to backroom intercession, execute that faithfully and He will bless you. Not everyone is called to be at the front or can take the pressure that comes with leadership. Show your face in the place and God will take His place.

Who is that person at your church that has dedicated their prayer time solely for lifting up the hands of the leadership of your church? Be that one. You are reading about Father Nash today because his prayers helped to bring the revival as Finney's intercessor and this shows you how important he was.

Sialkot Revival

John Nelson Hyde (1865 - 1912) was an American missionary who preached in the Punjab. He helped to found the Punjab Prayer Union. He was a man who was always on his knees, that is why he was known as 'Praying Hyde'. You know you are a prayer addict when prayer becomes your second name. Praying Hyde and his friends would set aside half an hour per day to fast and pray for revival in India.

These prayers preceded the Sialkot awakening in India, which began in 1904 in Sialkot and led to the salvation of many people. It is reported that Praying Hyde, during the course of the revival, was constantly in the prayer room.

Azusa Street Revival (1906-1911)

William Joseph Seymour (1870 - 1908) is the man whom God chose to spearhead the Azusa Street, Pentecostal revival. He was a thirty-five-year-old African American, a son of slaves who had one eye. This shows you that God does not discriminate; He can use anyone, in any way, and anywhere, as long as they're are willing to be used by Him. I highlight this revival because Seymour was a man of prayer!

History records that this man was always praying and fasting. Before the revival came down, Seymour had declared ten days of fasting and prayer. My friends, can you see what the cradle of revival was? The folks at Azusa began to speak in tongues and started to see great healing, and people from far and wide came to experience and receive the Holy Ghost baptism. Seymour himself received the baptism of the Holy Ghost after praying all night long!

Do you need the Holy Ghost? Ever thought of praying all night long? Well, there is a pattern here with what

A Key Ingredient of Revival

happened in Acts 2. Prayer was integral.

Let us pray: Dear Lord, revive us again! We repent of any sins and transgressions as we lay our hearts on the altar. We call upon Your name as we humble ourselves. We give away our desires and wishes and submit them to Your will. Bring healing to our land, bring restoration, let there be an awakening. We want to see Your healing and saving power transform this nation again. This nation needs You now more than ever. Raise up some intercessors that are willing to get on their knees and call upon You day and night. Let there be a mighty outpouring of the Holy Spirit. In Jesus name we pray.

Amen.

As we reflect on the stories and lessons in this chapter, remember that revival starts with you. Your dedication to prayer can ignite a flame that touches many.

Reflection and Application
Chapter 5: A Key Ingredient of Revival

1. Personal Prayer and Revival: How do you currently approach prayer in your daily life? What changes can you make to move from simply praying for revival to becoming a vessel of revival, as described in this chapter?

_____

_____

_____

2. Commitment to Consistent Prayer: The chapter shares examples of great prayer warriors like Aimee Semple McPherson and Father Nash. What lessons can you take from their dedication to prayer?

_____

_____

_____

_____

3. Creating Your Own Revival Triangle: The 'Revival Triangle' includes prayer, the Word of God, and the Holy Spirit. Which of these elements do you need to focus on more in your life to ignite spiritual revival within and around you? What practical steps can you take to strengthen this aspect?

_____

_____

_____

_____

_____

_____

_____

_____

_____

_____

Chapter 6

Prayer as a Way of Life

When prayer becomes a **lifestyle**, it becomes a habit and a way of life. A habit is an acquired behavioural pattern, regularly followed until it becomes almost involuntary. Not all habits are sinful habits but if it is something undesirable, then you will seek to change it. In a Sunday sermon, I spoke about how to break bad habits. I mentioned that one of the ways to break a bad habit is to replace it with another habit. This is from Psalm 119:11, where David says, "I have hid thy Word in my heart so I will not sin against God". In this case, David is saying that instead of habouring sin, such as lust, doubt and negative thoughts in your heart, replace them with the Word of God. If you have any habits you do not like, replace them with prayer and fasting, with God's help.

We are in a world where **a lifestyle of prayer** is getting out of fashion and other alternative lifestyles are highly fashionable. The believer has to stand out from the crowd and be counted on the Lord's side. It is when we fit in with the crowd that we lose relevance and influence. We are products of influence directly or indirectly. Many of the things that you do are because someone negatively or positively influenced you. True leaders lead by influence of their example. Let your life do the talking by being a living witness of the Lord. Imagine how many people you can influence simply by your daily routine? Prayer is the **lifestyle** and currency of the spiritually rich and successful in Christ.

Prioritising Prayer

Do you use prayer as much as you should? Here is a test. Whenever you are faced with any difficulty or trouble, who and where do you turn to instinctively? What is your priority in life? If your spouse mistreats you, what do you do first? Do you pick up the phone and tell a friend, or do you say a quick word of prayer?

I was driving my car alone one day. The road was icy, and it had been snowing for a few days. Suddenly, out of nowhere, I lost control of the vehicle. It started to slide on the slippery road. I was terrified, especially since there were other cars in the roundabout. All I did was slam on the brake as hard as I could and shout, "JESUS!"

The moment that I called on Jesus, something miraculous happened. My vehicle swerved well out of the junction and halted to a stop on the next exit.

I believe that God helped me because I called on His Name as His word says. My point here is, if you were in a really tight situation, what would be your instinctive reaction? This is a way to see if prayer is near you. Some would have sworn or just screamed if that happened to them. I am saying here that if prayer is a **lifestyle**, you will always have Christ on the foremost of your mind. If you are faced with a medical emergency, who do you call first, Jesus or the ambulance? Human help has limitations, that is why Jesus Christ should be your first and unconscious port of call.

God told my wife and I that we would lead a group of people and our theme would be 'We are a people of prayer'. We do not want to be known as the biggest group or the wealthiest group or most popular; we want to be known for prayer. We envisioned prayer hubs being erected throughout the country. In these centres, when one enters, they can see the Cloud of Glory when the people begin to pray.

Safeguarding Your Prayer Life

When you set yourself as a person of prayer, people will not distract you with trivial matters. If a friend calls and wants to talk about someone else in the church, as a person of prayer, you will respond by saying, "We need to pray about it." On many occasions, we put ourselves as people open to jesting and gossip, which is why we cannot reign in on pressure from colleagues. When prayer envelops your life, you do not have time to waste because your time is spent praying. You do not have bad words to say about others because your words are spent in prayer. You do not have any energy to do mischief because your energy is sent in prayer.

You have to safeguard your prayer life with your life. There will always be distractions to try and take you away from prayer, but when you commit to making prayer a priority it will become automatic. You can eat too much, you can sing too much, you can run too much, you can talk too much but you can never pray too much. If this is your policy in life, you will learn to give prayer the time it deserves. You will also have to appreciate that **a lifestyle of prayer** is a lifestyle of sacrifice. Sacrificing some of the things you may want to do in exchange for communion with God. Those who sacrifice more than others in life often live the kind of life that those who do not sacrifice will envy.

The reason why you need to guard your prayer life with everything you have is because that is where the power of a believer lies. No prayer is equivalent to no power. More prayer equals more power. Remember Samson who was a Judge over Israel and had taken a Nazirite vow; set apart for God. When Samson started sharing his time between God and a lady called Delilah, he started to lose his power. There will always be Delilahs near your life, seeking to take your power away by keeping you away from prayer. Do not let them succeed. Now that we understand the importance of guarding our prayer time, let's explore the perseverance needed in prayer.

Pray Again

When you become a person given to prayer, you will realise that you can never over pray. Even Jesus teaches us that if at first your prayer does not do exactly as you were expecting, you need to pray again. Matthew 26:44 tells us that when Jesus was praying in the garden, He prayed the same prayer three times. Keep on praying friend, Jesus did the same. You can eat too much, drink too much, sleep too much, run too much, laugh too much but you can never pray too much.

In Mark 8, we read the story of a blind man for whom Jesus prayed twice. Now, remember I said earlier in this book that prayer changes things but if it does not change things, it changes the way you see things. This is what happened here. Jesus prayed for him and after the prayer, He asked him if he can see. This here is an example of faith and expectation, after you pray for something, check it. The blind man was asked how his eyesight was after the prayer and he said, "I see men as trees walking". Here, God did not heal him totally but actually changed the way he saw his problem. His problem was that all he could see was total darkness. After prayer, God changed his dim view on his situation. He could see trees walking now. I pray that God may change the way you see your problem. Amen. On the second prayer, the man was totally healed and this is because Jesus prayed again! Never be ashamed to pray again or to pray too much, this is what Jesus teaches us.

Intercessory Prayer

I believe that every church needs an intercessory group. We have a great example from the church in Acts 12, when they prayed for Peter until he was released. My wife leads our faithful intercessory team and once shared some useful insights on intercession. Everyone should really be an intercessor, but you will find that when you have a core group of people that are passionate about it and are called by God, it is more of a blessing and easy to manage.

The prayer of intercession can be defined by observing the word 'intercede'. To intercede means to act between two parties in order to reconcile the two of them. Therefore, the prayer of intercession is standing in the gap in prayer on behalf of another.

> *Who is he that condemneth? It is Christ that died, yea rather, that is risen again, who is even at the right hand of God, who also maketh intercession for us.*
>
> **(Romans 8:34)**

The verse above shows us what intercession is and that Jesus is our prime example. He sits on the right hand of God amplifying any prayer that we make before the throne. When you pray, you need to pray to the Father, just like Jesus taught us in the Lord's Prayer. He interceded for us. So, the right way is pray to God the heavenly Father, in the name of Jesus Christ the Son, through the help and guidance of the Holy Ghost. There we have it; the Godhead has been given their rightful positions in prayer.

The Qualities of an Intercessor

In order for you to be an effective intercessor, you need to have the following qualities:

1. **Selflessness** – This is the art of being unselfish. You cannot be selfish in prayer. Philippians 2:4 instructs us not to focus solely on our own issues but to also take into account the needs and concerns of others.
2. **Humility** – My definition of true humility is when someone accepts God's will for their life and walks in it. Die to self. Die to your own wishes and desires of what and how you think you should pray, as elaborated by the following verses.

> *Trust in the Lord with all your heart, And lean not on your own understanding; In all your ways acknowledge Him, And He shall direct your paths.*
>
> **(Proverbs 3:5-6)**

> *He who trusts in his own heart is a fool, but whoever walks wisely will be delivered.*
>
> **(Proverbs 28:26)**

3. **Coming clean before the Lord** – Your prayers will

not be heard if there is unconfessed sin in your heart, such as bitterness and unforgiveness according to Psalm 66:18. *The Lord will not hear me if I hold on to sin in my heart.*

4. **Dedication and commitment** – You will find that if you have a cause or prayer point that you really believe in, or are passionate about, you will pray about it with more dedication. Intercession is like the claws of an Eagle. When an Eagle clenches its claws it does not let go. When you are called to pray for something, you cannot dilly dally or leave it until it is completed. You have to hold on in Faith and P.U.S.H (Pray Until Something Happens.) Many people promise you they are going to pray for you but never pray. Intercessors are not like that, if they promise to pray, they will do it.

5. **Expectation** – Expectation is the mother of manifestation. (Romans 8:25). If you have been praying for something, check on progress.

Times We Should Pray

I deeply love my beautiful wife, Josie, and enjoy the intimate relationship we share. The relationship we have affords me to talk to her anytime during the day. I know she is just a phone call or text message away, and I don't have to limit our conversations to lunch or any specific time. I practically talk to her throughout the day. This is how we effectively run the businesses and organisations we lead – constant communication.

Many religions have set hours and times of prayer engraved as rules. Muslims have what is called the *'Salat'* prayer. This is an obligatory prayer that has to be done five times a day. Sikhs on the other hand have a code of conduct that instructs them to pray daily, three hours before dawn.

If we go back to the Bible era, there were three times dedicated for prayer in a day. These were; the Third Hour (9am), the Sixth Hour (12noon), and Ninth Hour (3pm). The prophet Daniel in the Bible prayed three times a day. We know even the Apostles in Acts are said to frequent the temple to pray at the hours of prayer. When the Holy Ghost came down in the Upper Room it was at the hour of prayer. The reason why these set times of prayer were kept is so that people do not forget to pray and pray without ceasing. Of course, the origins of this practice and pattern stem from a Judaic heritage. This book wants to show you a more excellent way of praying without ceasing.

If prayer becomes ascribed to a set time as a rule, then it is not partnership with God, it just becomes a practice. I am not saying one must not be disciplined and set aside some time for God. No. I am saying prayer must not be a job, it must be a joy!

Why pray three times a day only, when you can pray continually through the day? Relationship with the Father allows us direct access to the throne of Grace twenty-four hours a day. Let me share with you some true stories on how praying as a way of life has yielded results.

Steam Train is Halted Due to Prayer

A lifestyle of prayer will allow you to be in control of situations that arise in your daily life even on the trot. I read a story about a testimony of the power of a lifestyle of prayer which happened in 1864. A lady was travelling with her elderly and disabled father, and two young daughters. Their steam train was delayed by over an hour. They asked their train conductors to speed up the train so they could catch the train ahead and the conductors told them that it was impossible to get there on time. The earliest would be half an hour late. The reason why they wanted to get there on time was because if they missed the train, that means they would have to sleep outside in the freezing cold and freeze to death. While on this train, she started to pray unto God and said, "O God, if thou art my Father, and I am thy child, put it into the heart of that conductor to wait till we get there". After saying this prayer, she fell asleep and forgot about it.

When they got to the place where they were going to change over trains, to their amazement the train was waiting for them. Do you see the power of **a lifestyle of prayer** my friend? Pray on the go as and when you need it. The conductor confessed that he had never done it before in his life, to wait that long for something that he did not know. A feeling just told him that he had to wait for something pending and he waited. The family of four got home safe and sound!

Praying in Tongues Results in a Miracle

I read a story about a 60-year-old American grandmother in Michigan who was attacked by armed intruders. They entered her house at 4am and demanded money from her husband. They wound duct tape around her ankles, wrists, eyes, and mouth. She was kidnapped and away they sped with her. She was threatened to keep her head down or she will be killed. This lady trusted in God and was a Christian, but at this point she did not even think about praying because of the trauma and confusion of it all. She said the turning point was when she remembered to call unto the Lord.

This lady said she focused on God and that was when things changed. Things did not change in her situation, as she was still in the back of this car, things changed in her heart.

As she was too stunned to utter words in English, she started to pray in tongues. She admitted that praying in the spirit helped her talk to God, as she didn't know what to pray. She said the duct tape kept her mouth shut but could not keep her tongue from moving. As she prayed, she felt her body relaxing. The shocking story of her abduction and subsequent miracle rescue started after she began to pray in the spirit. Prayer works!

Insight From Prayer

Numerous times, I have stood before people who were total strangers to me, needing me to minister to them one way or the other. This could be in a healing prayer line or even in a one-to-one counselling setting. God will reveal to me things about their life that I had no idea of knowing at all. This is just the grace of God. Now, this advice may help you and sharpen your ability to hear from God even more. Usually, what most ministers tend to do is just rush things and start to minister to them, be it in prayer or prophecy, without asking God first. You have not, because you ask not. If you ask Him at that moment, He can give you what He wills at that moment. I always wait upon the Lord and even commence a conversation with the person while waiting for an answer from the Lord. This is because secretly, in my spirit, I am praying at that very moment. I would ask God to reveal something that can help bring a solution to their issue or to raise their faith. It always works!

A Challenge

As we conclude this chapter, remember that prayer is not just an activity but a way of life. It is the heartbeat of your relationship with God, the fuel that sustains your spirit and strengthens your faith. Just as you wouldn't go a day without breathing, make prayer an essential part of your daily routine. Let it become your second nature; a seamless, continuous conversation with your Creator.

This week, commit to incorporating prayer into your routine so that it becomes as natural as breathing. Start by dedicating short moments throughout your day to pause and connect with God. Whether you're driving, working, or relaxing, let prayer be your immediate response in all situations. Remember, the power of a prayer-filled life is not found in long, eloquent words but in the heart that constantly seeks God's presence.

Reflection and Application
Chapter 6: Prayer as a Way of Life

---

1. Examining Your Instinctive Reactions: When faced with challenges or moments of crisis, what is your first instinct? Do you turn to prayer, or do you rely on your own strength or human solutions?

_____

_____

_____

2. Prioritising and Safeguarding Your Prayer Life: What steps can you take to ensure that prayer becomes a protected and essential part of your daily routine, even amidst life's busyness?

_____

_____

_____

_____

3. Adopting Prayer as a Habit: The chapter discusses prayer as a lifestyle and habitual practice. What practical changes can you make to integrate prayer more naturally into your day-to-day activities so that it becomes an involuntary and continuous part of your life?

_____

_____

_____

_____

_____

_____

_____

_____

_____

_____

Chapter 7

Praying Nonstop

1 Thessalonians 5:17 tells us that we need to pray without ceasing. I have found myself again having to resort for help in Greek during my study time. I wanted to get an understanding of the term *without ceasing* in the Bible. The Greek word is *adialeiptos* pronounced as {ad-ee-al-ipe'-toce}. This word is used four times in the New Testament and every time it is used, it is in conjunction with prayer. Here are the other places it is used.

For God is my witness, whom I serve with my spirit in the gospel of his Son, that without ceasing I make mention of you always in my prayers;

(Romans 1:9)

*We give thanks to God always for you all,
making mention of you in our prayers.*

(1 Thessalonians 1:2)

For this cause also thank we God without ceasing, because, when ye received the word of God which ye heard of us, ye received it not as the word of men, but as it is in truth, the word of God, which effectually worketh also in you that believe.

(1 Thessalonians 2:13)

*Adialeiptos*is is used to describe something that is done incessantly, without intermission, continually, always, Uninterruptedly, and without omission. For example: regular consistent production of fruit, a persistent cough or repeated military attacks. I can assure you that whenever you pray, you are sending artillery to the camp of the enemy.

This means we have to be praying nonstop. How is it possible that someone can pray without ceasing? As you know, we have to go to work, eat, sleep and do other things in life, making it nearly impossible to pray nonstop. In this book, I want to show you how this is possible. Yes, it is possible because God will not ask us to do things that are impossible.

The Power of the Mind

When God created us, He gave us a very powerful thing called the mind. Science has not yet been able to tap in to see everything about the power of the mind. Some experts say that we only use 10% of what our mind is built to do. Think about all the amazing inventions and man-made creations around us. I met a man a few months ago who could tell me what day of the week I was born, by just telling him my date of birth. He does it for anyone and never gets it wrong! The mind is amazing.

In the commercial world, companies invest heavily in subliminal advertising as it has been found to be very effective, as it actually deals with your mind directly. It has been outlawed in some countries. The New Age religion, Yoga, Hypnotism, and Spiritualist movements have now been exploring the mind and tapping into its outstanding power. However, I will need to caution you that unless you have the Holy Spirit, this is a slippery area to venture into. Let the Word of God be a standard always. The human mind was created by God and is awesome and I believe it can help us to pray without ceasing. It was created for His glory and purpose.

The Duality Within the Mind

I read an insightful book called the *The Power of Your Subconscious Mind*. The author states that the mind has two unique parts with different attributes and functions. The mind has a double nature, the conscious and the subconscious. Your conscious mind is your reasoning mind. It is the logical thinking part of your mind. It makes choices, such as which books you read, who your friends are, and where you want to go, etc.

On the other hand, your subconscious mind is the part of the mind that works without any conscious choice on your part. It takes care of things like breathing, salivating, and other vital things like digestion. Your subconscious mind simply works on what has been suggested by the conscious mind. This usually happens on autopilot. Your subconscious mind will accept anything that is sent to it whether right or wrong, real or fake.

The subconscious mind is like an ocean and anything can live in it. In an ocean, you can find bad creatures like killer whales, catfish, crabs, hairy frogfish, and good creatures like the rainbow trout. Your thoughts are like the animals that live and grow in there in the ocean. If you have bad thoughts they will continue to grow and thrive, these are the bad water creatures that devour the good fish in the ocean. This is why God's Word tells us to guard our minds, as you can read below.

> And the peace of God, which passeth all understanding, shall keep your hearts and minds through Christ Jesus.

(Philippians 4: 7)

The Repeater

Some time ago, an anointed lady friend came to minister for us and she sang a song called *Before you were born I knew you*, from Jeremiah. She sang this song at church on Sunday, and throughout the week, this song was repeating itself in my head! Every time it happened, I was blessed. I did not choose for that to happen but my subconscious mind took that song in when it was sung on Sunday, and it went on and on. Has that ever happened to you? The subconscious mind is also called the repeater. It can repeat things without your contribution. The subconscious mind does not get tired. This is the secret to twenty-four-hour prayer.

While your conscious mind is asleep, your subconscious mind is awake all the time! This is where your dreams at night come from. God also uses dreams to speak to us according to Job 33:14-15. This part of your mind has the ability to also meditate on God's promises and pray without ceasing!

What are you feeding your subconscious mind? TV? Radio? Negative words from naysayers? Worldly music? Remember that your mind will accept it, but it is not healthy. The mind is the ground where battles are either won or lost, guard it and keep it pure. Let the mind of Christ be in you. Think and see things through the eyes of Jesus Christ. What does He think about you and the situation that you are in?

A Fountain of Prayer

A fountain is a source. In order for you to be a fountain of prayer, your reservoir needs to be full. James 3:11 asks a pertinent question. Can both fresh water and salt water flow from the same fountain? The answer is 'No'. In order for you to be able to send forth powerful prayers like a fountain, your reservoir must be full of fresh water, which is the promises of God.

Meditation Prayers

Meditation on the Word of God will help you achieve **a lifestyle of prayer** without ceasing. Isaiah 26:3 tells us that God will keep you in perfect peace, if your MIND is fixed on Him. See what I mean? You really have to keep your mind on Jesus and there is no better way of doing it than keeping your mind on His Word. His Word is life. Meditate means to focus one's mind for a period of time. This is what a believer needs to do. Meditation is one of the things that Scripture instructs us to do.

This book of the law shall not depart out of thy mouth; but thou shalt meditate therein day and night, that thou mayest observe to do according to all that is written therein: for then thou shalt make thy way prosperous, and then thou shalt have good success.

(Joshua 1:8)

We should spend time on the Word. As you do that, your subconscious mind will take in all that the Word says and have it on auto replay. This is why praying in tongues builds up your spirit because it bypasses the conscious mind!

King David opens up the Psalms with a powerful chapter. He was a master at meditation.

Blessed is the man that walketh not in the counsel of the ungodly, nor standeth in the way of sinners, nor sitteth in the seat of the scornful. But his delight is in the law of the LORD; and in his law doth he meditate day and night. And he shall be like a tree planted by the rivers of water, that bringeth forth his fruit in his season; his leaf also shall not wither; and whatsoever he doeth shall prosper. The ungodly are not so: but are like the chaff which the wind driveth away. Therefore the ungodly shall not stand in the judgment, nor sinners in the congregation of the righteous. For the LORD knoweth the way of the righteous: but the way of the ungodly shall perish.

(Psalms 1: 1- 6)

Let me give you an example and a few things that you can do to help you meditate on the Word;

1. A good time to mediate on the Word is on your bed or in your bedroom! This can be done just before sleeping or first thing on waking up. This is what David did. *When I remember thee upon my bed, and Meditate on thee in the Night watches.* (Psalm 63:6)

2. Feed your subconscious mind with some stuff to work with. Biblical Psalms or a prayer is a good way to go. This can be in the form of a song, written or even spoken Word. There are many audio Bibles that you can acquire. You can get Scripture going around your head; the conscious mind may be tired or sleepy but remember the subconscious is always awake!

3. Watch a two-minute video with a Bible verse, or even a sermonette. There are loads of free ones on the internet. Repeat.

4. You may even take a simple short verse from the Bible, personalise, and memorise it. For example, Psalms 17:8 which reads: "Keep me as the apple of your eye; hide me in the shadow of your wings". What you do is, you speak it silently or out loud in your mind. You say, "You keep me (put your name) as the apple of your eye and hide me." Repeat this over and over. If you encounter an accidental situation during the day, those Words would serve as prayer in your subconscious mind.

5. You can even take a verse and write it down. Perhaps write it down in a way you understand. You can repeat this process to help you. If you do not fully understand a verse, look for its meaning until you understand it and can explain it; you are unlikely to forget it once you study and comprehend it. If you meet anyone share that verse.

I remember when I used to spend hours in 'prayer'. I would shut myself away and feel good that I had achieved many hours. If I didn't manage to clock my hours, I would feel guilty. This was because I used to view prayer as an episode. Then the Lord began to show me the revelation of what true prayer is. Prayer is not an event. Prayer should be a **lifestyle**! It's not about how long you have prayed or how loud; it's about constant and consistent communication with God.

Praying in the Spirit

> Likewise the Spirit also helpeth our infirmities: for we know not what we should pray for as we ought: but the Spirit itself maketh intercession for us with groanings which cannot be uttered.
>
> **(Romans 8:26)**

Praying in the Spirit is when your spirit man prays. This involves praying in tongues, groaning, and travailing. All are enriching ways of leading **a lifestyle of prayer**. Many times, when we are praying, we do not know how to do it in the way we should. We may know what we are praying for but unsure how to approach and present the issues before the throne of Grace. The scripture above discusses this and encourages us to pray in the spirit.

The Apostle Paul prayed much in tongues. In 1 Corinthians 14:18, he told the Corinthians that he spoke in tongues more than all of them. There is a reason why Paul, who walked in great power prayed in tongues, he knew the power that this kind of prayer releases. He was a Godly example to us as he set the church in order. Before we go further, I need to fine-tune a belief among some circles, which states that 'speaking in tongues is the initial evidence of receiving the baptism of the Holy Spirit.' Speaking in tongues can be, in some cases, a manifestation of receiving the Holy Spirit. However, this cannot be the sole proof.

I received the baptism of the Holy Spirit as a child on my tenth birthday. I did not speak in tongues on that day even though I really experienced an authentic touch from God that I cannot argue with. I felt His touch on my life. I cried uncontrollably like I have never done ever, my life changed. In fact, my Christian journey and destiny with God was sealed and aligned there. It was a little later in my Christian life that I spoke in tongues. Even as you are reading this right now, you might be asking God to fill you with the Holy Spirit. He is more willing to give it than you are to receive it. Just open your heart and say, "Lord, fill my cup", and He will do it.

My younger sister received the Holy Spirit while alone in her room. She knelt down on her bed and asked God to fill her and the next thing we saw and heard was her walking up and down the passageway of our house praising the Lord and thanking God for His power. He can do it for you, my friend. Just ask. I feel the presence of God even as I write this, and I pray that the same wind of Glory may blow over you, wherever you may be. God wants to use you for His glory, surrender your life to Him, do not worry what will happen when He comes on you, just open up and receive. If I had not had an experience of the Holy Spirit, you would have probably never heard of Joe Benjamin; I owe my whole life to Him and promise to serve Him all my days.

> *Howbeit when he, the Spirit of truth, is come, he will guide you into all truth: for he shall not speak of himself; but whatsoever he shall hear, that shall he speak: and he will shew you things to come.*

(John 16:13)

The evidence of receiving the Holy Spirit is that it will lead you to all truth, according to Jesus Christ in the verse above. The Holy Spirit will lead you to the gospel truth of your generation. Remember that the Bible says that the elect cannot be deceived. When you receive the Holy Spirit, you receive the spirit of truth, enabling you to discern and distinguish truth from error. The baptism of the Holy Spirit is not just an event; it is an ongoing experience. Hence, it cannot happen without you not knowing. Look at some examples; the disciples in the Upper Room (Acts 2), and the disciples at Ephesus (Acts 19:6).

The reason I digress is because you cannot speak about tongues and not address the Holy Spirit. On the subject of tongues, Paul also says that not everyone has these gifts of the Spirit but exhorts us to earnestly desire these gifts. Just because you have never spoken in tongues does not mean you do not have the Holy Spirit. If you have never spoken in tongues but have the desire, you need to ask God who is the giver of every good gift. Do not be afraid of what will happen when you receive it. The Holy Spirit is sweet and gentle like a dove. Let go and let Him have His way.

The primary misconception about tongues is that many people fail to understand there are two distinct types of tongues. Firstly, there is the praying in tongues (speaking in tongues) unto the Lord. This does not need any interpretation because God understands anything uttered in the spirit (1 Corinthians 14:14-15). This is the level or prayer that any believer can tap into and they will realise how easy it is to pray. There is so much grace and glory released when this interaction with God in the spirit happens.

Secondly, there is the Gift of speaking in tongues which is available to only some. Paul calls it the speaking of diverse tongues in 1 Corinthians 12:10. This needs to be interpreted because it is usually a message to the church, not a personal prayer to God. In this gift, God is speaking through the vessel and it will need interpretation so that the people can understand what God is saying. Paul also set some order on how this gift should be operated in church services.

A Lifestyle of Prayer

For if I pray in an unknown tongue, my spirit prayeth, but my understanding is unfruitful. What is it then? I will pray with the spirit, and I will pray with the understanding also: I will sing with the spirit, and I will sing with the understanding also.

(1 Corinthians 14:14-15)

The verse above states that there is a difference between praying in tongues and praying with understanding (the language that you comprehend i.e. English). Praying with understanding is like riding a bicycle, while praying in tongues is like riding a motorbike. With a bicycle, you have to do most of the work, such as pedalling, to keep it moving. However, with a motor bike, all you need to do is ensure you're securely seated, and the motor bike propels you forward at a much faster speed. The benefit of praying in the spirit is, you do not have to figure anything out or make sentences, as this can be wearisome. God knows what we are going to say even before we say it. With praying in the spirit, you can detach yourself from the process and let the spirit take over. This means you can pray longer periods, as the things on your heart are released by the Spirit.

How do you pray when you do not know how to pray? I remember one time I was in my study and I had some real deep weights on my heart. I wanted to pray to God but it was so heavy that I could not say it all. It felt as though those burdens just made me cry out to God with no words, expressing myself through sighs and groans. I was in travail and the prayer of travailing produces crying, groaning, and sighs. It is okay sometimes to groan in His presence, where maybe there might be instances of grief or sorrow. There are many examples in the Bible where prayers went up to God as groans. People like David said, "Lord, my groaning is not hid from thee".

We know Jesus, when He was at Lazarus' grave groaned before he called Lazarus, alive, out of the grave. This is spiritual travail and usually happens when something is about to be born. As you know, before a mother gives birth she will go through a period of labour. The birth pains are not for her, they are so that the baby can be born. Many times, when we are in travail, we are just intercessors for something that is going to be born. God wants to birth something through the womb of your prayer and may place a burden so hard on you that you groan until that baby is born. Stay on your knees keep pushing, sighing, and groaning and you will see God's will for your life come into full manifestation.

Reflection and Application
Chapter 7: Praying Nonstop

Understanding Continuous Prayer: What steps can you take to make prayer an uninterrupted part of your life, as described in 1 Thessalonians 5:17?

_____

_____

_____

Guarding Your Mind and Spirit: The chapter mentions the importance of what you feed your subconscious mind. What adjustments can you make to ensure that your mind is filled with God's Word and not with negative or worldly influences?

_____

_____

_____

_____

Experiencing Deep Spiritual Prayer: Have you had moments when you prayed deeply, such as praying in the Spirit or groaning in intercession? Reflect on how these experiences impacted your faith, and think about how you can create opportunities to connect with God at this deeper level in your prayer life.

_____

_____

_____

_____

_____

_____

_____

_____

_____

_____

Chapter 8

Practical Prayer Ideas

Remember that prayer is communing to almighty God. In order to make it a **lifestyle**, you really need to be consistent at it. Imagine if we asked God's opinion about our day-to-day issues and decisions twenty-four hours a day, we would never get anything wrong. I want to share practical and applicable ways you can use in your daily life to pray and make it enjoyable at the same time.

Prayer Run or Walk

A few years back, while at a friend's house, we ended up playing energetic football in their garden. After thirty minutes of running up and about with the guys and having fun, I realised I ran out of breath. It was severe to the extent that I started to feel light headed. I sat down to rest and get my breath back, but I simply had no more strength in my body to continue playing ball. I then discovered that I was not as fit as I thought I was. My body was just about to shut down from just one hour of physical activity. I really had to do something about this. Something had to change.

Many times, we, as Christians, think we are fit but when your prayer muscles are put to the test, they fail. You spiritual fitness is only as strong as your prayer life. It is your response to a prayer call that can tell us how fit you are spiritually. When you start to pray and five minutes into your prayer you feel faint, then you know you need to do something to strengthen your spiritual muscles. Christ has called us to pray and not faint.

*And he spake a parable unto them to this end,
that men ought always to pray, and not to faint;*

(Luke 18:1)

Physical exercise does to the body what prayer does to your spirit man. When you exercise your muscles, it makes them grow stronger. When you exercise your prayer muscles, you will grow to be a spiritual giant. Lack of prayer in your life makes you a bunch of spiritual weak bones.

Science tells us that when we exercise our bodies, we release hormones called endorphins. These endorphins are responsible for your mood. They are known to reduce stress and trigger feelings of happiness. Wow, is God not amazing and so great that He created the body in this fashion? Another benefit of these endorphins is that they enhance the immune response. There you go again, as I have said earlier, prayer exercise does the same to your spirit. It reduces stress and pain, it makes you feel happier, and strengthens your immunity to sin.

There is a section of Christians that are against physical exercise. Their conviction comes from Paul's assertion that bodily exercise has little profit, which is found in 1 Timothy 4:8. However, in this Scripture, Paul actually concedes that there is some profit. However, the profit is not as much as compared to godliness which benefits the present life and your future life. Body exercise helps us in this life, not in the life to come because we will get a body change. We need to seek the kingdom first and make that our priority. Don't just be a physical fitness fanatic when your spiritual life is weak. However, our bodies are the temple of the Holy Spirit. In order for us to be good stewards of our temples, we need to take care of them! Like Paul says:

A Lifestyle of Prayer

What? know ye not that your body is the temple of the Holy Ghost which is in you, which ye have of God, and ye are not your own? For ye are bought with a price: therefore glorify God in your body, and in your spirit, which are God's.

(1 Corinthians 6:19-20)

Because something in my life had to change, to help me get fit, I decided to go on a daily exercise regime, where I do at least half an hour of running or cycling daily. The key here is to be praying while running. I found this to be both a benefit to the physical man and spirit man. Sometimes, when running, I pray in the Spirit; other times, I pray through song. As I run and pray, I get a chance to also hear what God is saying back to me. We learnt from the Bible that Enoch of old walked with God. We walk with our dogs, spouses, and kids but do we ever walk with God? We are encouraged to walk by faith; He is with us and in us to the end of the world. Walking by faith is walking with God, because when there is no faith, we cannot make God happy.

Find an exercise or hobby that you can include in your daily routine and tie it up with prayer. While you are playing tennis, golf, gardening, dancing, swimming, in the gym, walking or even housework, make sure you do not waste that important time as it could also be your prayer time. See how easy it is to pray without ceasing!

Family Altar

Growing up, I can't recall a day that passed without our family gathering for the family altar. My Dad would read a short Bible verse, and then we would all kneel and pray. I believe it is those prayers, instilled in us from a young age, that have shaped us into the people we are today. We were a family of seven children, but we had a set time that we had to all assemble in the lounge for family prayer. This was either first thing in the morning or last thing before we went to bed.

Families are breaking apart because the cement that holds families together, called prayer, is nonexistent. The house is in chaos because families do not have any daily routines. Schools have daily routines and kids know how to follow those routines. There must be some form of routine in the home that includes prayer. Prayer has been outlawed in schools but should not be outlawed in Christian homes too. Couples that live together as well, perhaps with no children in the home, should have times of praying together. In our marital counselling sessions, one of the best pieces of advice I give to married couples, is to set a time in the day when they can spend some minutes of the in prayer. I do not see how you both can say amen and start arguing after that!

We used to sing a little song:

> *Don't forget the family prayer*
> *Jesus wants to meet you there*
> *He will take your every care*
> *Don't forget the family prayer*

Prayer Book

When I got married, my beautiful wife created a Prayer Book. It had three sections: Date, Prayer Request, and Date Answered. Whenever we got an issue that we were sincerely praying for, we would place it in the Prayer Book and date when we asked God and when He answered our prayer. I have just looked at that prayer book and I can tell you that every prayer that we asked of God was ticked off and dated as answered! Praise the Lord! This is the power of prayer and also the blessing of journaling. You can look back and see that for sure God has been good. The power of putting your prayer in a book is also that it activates your faith and expectation. When you pray, you look for the answer. I also believe that every time we wrote down the request, even though we may have not knelt down to pray for it, God saw it and honoured it as a prayer.

Practical Prayer Ideas

We have one phone line that is dedicated for prayer in our home. We have had this going ever since my beautiful wife, Josie, told me that she had a burden for intercession. So, when we started this, we created a Prayer Book that she uses to enter the name of the person requesting prayer and their request. This way, we know what we have to pray for. This is a good thing to do even as an individual. You can open a private prayer book where you write down your requests and follow them up when answered. Keep it and see God answer your every request. God answers every prayer with a resounding yes, a not yet, or with a better answer than you anticipated.

Prayer Points

On many occasions, when one is in prayer, focus is difficult because one may have many things to pray about and it is easy to forget some things. Creating a prayer list with prayer points is a good way to stay focused.

For example, you can write:

1. Pray for cousin in the hospital.
2. Pray for job interview.
3. Pray for peace in Jerusalem.
4. Pray for more wisdom and a closer walk with the Lord.

This is one easy way to pray for an extended time without sounding repetitive or losing focus. Feel free to pause, pick a prayer point, and give it some minutes. I find this approach works well for small groups and even during family prayer. We regularly do this in church during our time of prayer. The person leading the prayer waits upon the Lord for prayer points and calls them out. The congregation rallies around those in fervent prayer.

Prayer Music

Prayer and meditation music helps you soak into the presence of God. It detaches you from your immediate environment and takes you higher with God.

I acquired some serene Christian instrumental music that lasts over an hour. Whenever we are about to have our family prayer, I play this music and dim the lights. My children, who are four and two, already recognise from the music that it is prayer time. Jair, of course starts praying in tongues, mimicking me.

I find meditation and prayer music great for the praying atmosphere and also keeps you zoned in your place of prayer. You can find different types of free prayer music online. Try it and see if it will not make you pray more deeply and intensely. In the Bible, we see an example of how the Spirit of the Lord came upon Elisha when the musician started to play.

> But now bring me a minstrel. And it came to pass, when the minstrel played, that the hand of the LORD came upon him.

(2 Kings 3:15)

Online Prayers

Listening to or participating in prayer audios and videos, whether live or recorded, is an excellent way to stay connected with God. This method has proven to be highly effective for maintaining a committed prayer life. In 2024, God inspired me to start the *Global Prayer Zone* movement on YouTube. This is an example of corporate prayer, bringing together individuals from various locations, united for a common purpose. We have gathered daily for months, impacting the lives of thousands through this initiative. To benefit from such experiences, make a commitment to align your prayer schedule with an online prayer hour and join others in the powerful act of agreement. Remember, distance is never a barrier in spiritual matters. Seek out an online prayer community that resonates with you, it can greatly enhance your prayer life.

Prayer Wall

Each year, we invite our friends and ministry partners to send us their prayer requests. I have a special prayer wall in my study where we pin the requests with thumbtack. Josie and I then take time to pray over them as often as we can. Sometimes, we simply call out the names of the people in prayer while facing that wall. Sometimes, we stick Bible verses there and when we are praying, we just glance at Scripture and recite it. We also use this wall to stick pictures of things that we are believing God for. Last year, we were trusting God for a particular vehicle, Josie looked for the car picture in a car magazine, cut it out and stuck it on the prayer wall. Every time we prayed, we saw it and it activated our faith and gave us a real picture of what to pray for. Not long before the end of the year, God graciously granted us the desire of our heart, brand new! He saw the requests on our prayer wall. As I speak, that wall is plastered with prayer requests from all our partners and friends worldwide. I got this revelation from Isaiah. Scripture suggests that he had a wall that he would pray facing. "Hezekiah turned his face toward the wall, and prayed unto the LORD" (Isaiah 38:2).

Prayer Partner

The word of the Lord declares that where there are two or three gathered in His Name, He is duty bound to be present. Many times, prayer feels like a lonely affair because you are doing it alone. It is a good idea to look for someone whom you can pray with. Statistics show that people who are trying to lose weight are more likely to lose weight if they are part of a group, like *weight watchers* rather than going it alone. Some people need company to encourage them and keep them going as they struggle praying alone. At one point, even Jesus asked His disciples to give Him moral support for prayer.

> And he cometh unto the disciples, and findeth them asleep, and saith unto Peter, What, could ye not watch with me one hour?
>
> **(Matthew 26:40)**

If you know about a prayer meeting in your area, be a part of it. Every time you go there, you get revived and rejuvenated. Do not stay home when the saints are gathering.

When you choose your prayer partner, make sure you find someone who has the same burden for prayer as you do. People will either break you or build you. You can also have things that you both maybe passionate about. For example, praying for the persecuted church. This makes the bond stronger and your chemistry amazing. The other benefit of prayer partnerships is that you become accountable to each other, and to God of course.

Corporate Prayer

God told me that whenever we meet for our services, we should open them up with prayer. Many times, people sit in churches and talk about the weather, or the makeup they are wearing, and it ends up being more of a social gathering than a spiritual one. In these last days, the church really needs to embrace prayer back in the house of the Lord. When we open the meeting with corporate prayer all together, this actually changes the atmosphere. Prayer changes the temperature of the room. We have it in our power to change the altitude when we gather! People come home stressed and tired, but prayer always brings a refreshing. This is what we hold dear as culture in our church and it has been a great blessing.

Paul encourages us to always be found where believers are gathered. Corporate prayer is also a great time to talk to God. Jesus, in Matthew 6:6, says that when you pray at home in your prayer closet, you should shut the door and pray. I understand that many people see prayer as a private thing and shy away from praying out loud in church. However, this is not the same requirement when we pray together as one body corporately in church or in a prayer meeting.

Corporate prayer is not really meant to be only personal. It is not about YOU, it is about US. Look at how Jesus taught us how to pray corporately in the Lord's Prayer. It generally says, 'US' not 'ME'.

> *After this manner therefore pray ye: Our Father which art in heaven, Hallowed be thy name. Thy kingdom come. Thy will be done in earth, as it is in heaven. Give US this day our daily bread. And forgive US our debts, as WE forgive our debtors. And lead US not into temptation, but deliver US from evil: For thine is the kingdom, and the power, and the glory, for ever. Amen.*
>
> **(Matthew 6:9-13)**

Praying at Midnight

Psalm 91:5 says that you shall not fear the terror by night. We see that the devil sometimes would like to use nighttime to bring terror and fear. Ephesians also warns us against the works of darkness. Alcoholics get drunk like a sponge at night, the night clubs and red-light districts come to life at night. Nocturnal animals like owls, bats, and foxes all come to life. Burglars, rapists, and murders love to operate at night. It is well known in African witchcraft that the witches love to work at night. They ride distances of many miles on flying saucers and broomsticks. The reason why they choose nighttime is to avoid detection. It can be said that there is an increased presence and activity of demonic forces in the night hours of the day. Even people who suffer from long term oppressions, like depression and anxiety, actually suffer most oppression at night.

Torment, extreme insomnia, and nightmares do not come from the Lord. However, you will notice that sometimes God wants your attention and may cause you to feel uneasy and somehow nervous. A regular occurrence in my life is that some nights, even after a long day, I put my head on the pillow but I cannot get any sleep, yet I am tired. I may feel a bit nervous and tense, and then get up from my bed and go into my study. As I sit at my desk,

God will start to speak to me. He may tell me what I have to preach or about different issues affecting people I need to pray for. I lose all sense of time in that presence of God. When I finish talking to Him, I go back to bed and sleep soundly like a baby! Unfortunately, Josie would have a hard time trying to wake me up the next morning.

Many times, when God wants your attention, He gives

you a gentle nudge which can be in the form of taking your sleep away temporarily. When you give God you attention, He then gives you direction. Sometimes, spiritual warfare is raging at night, and God wants you to wake up and pray.

Young Samuel served under the High Priest Eli when the Lord appeared to young Samuel at night. The story of Samuel in 1 Samuel 3 reaffirms the importance of having good spiritual fathers who can help sons grow in the Lord and also teach them to hear God's voice. Sometimes, regrettably, because of our zeal and enthusiasm, we run when we do not have any mentorship and training and that is why we falter. There are two ways to learn in life; by making mistakes or by mentors – you get to choose. Mentors help you avoid the pitfalls they have been through and you become wiser. It was night and Samuel was about to go to sleep, but God wanted to talk to him. It took his mentor to recognise and teach Samuel how to respond to God's voice.

Get yourself under some Godly leadership and let someone teach you how to pray and walk closer to the Lord. Samuel wanted to sleep but could not sleep as he kept hearing God's voice. Understand that God's voice to you can come in almost any shape or form and at any time. God's voice to you can also be through your spiritual leadership. When Samuel was able to listen and obey the voice of his High Priest, he was able to hear and obey God's voice. If you do not know how to pray, ask someone. Eventually, Samuel realised that the reason why he could not sleep was because God had a message for him. He said, "Speak my Lord". You need to be willing to say 'Speak my Lord'; this is **a lifestyle of prayer** and communion with God. Never be too busy or too tired to hear from God.

In Acts 16:25-34, we read about Paul and Silas praying at midnight, until there was a great earthquake. What this proves to me is that while nighttime is a time where demons are active, this is also a time where angels are active! You must never be afraid of the night or nightmares because greater is He that is in you! When the evil spirits are floating about, the Holy Spirit is also watching over you.

Another day I was asleep and God made me aware of a situation that was happening to a lady I know in a night vision. Instantly, I woke up and started to pray for her. When I spoke to her later, she confirmed she was under an attack and that spiritual intervention was an encouragement to her. Whenever you have a vision, thought, or even a feeling about someone or some situation, you need to get up and pray about it even when it is at night.

There are many references in the Bible about midnight. However, midnight is not strictly meaning 0000hours.

This can be anytime a couple of hours after midnight. The Bible speaks a lot about praying at night, and David in the Old Testament used to pray at night. This is because God never sleeps! Actually, you may find that, when everything is quiet and tranquil, is a better time to pray. If you have chopped-up sleep, do not see that as a completely negative thing. Use it, because there is power at midnight, as David teaches us in the verse below.

At midnight I will rise to give thanks unto thee because of thy righteous judgments.

(Psalm 119:62)

A Light Shines in Our Bedroom

One time, my lovely wife and I were in bed at night. As we were lying on the bed, I started to sense a presence in our bedroom. It was pitch dark, as it was in the middle of winter and we did not have any lights switched on, inside or outside our bedroom. I told Josie that God's Angels were present in the room. I could see a round white light which was gently glowing in a corner of our room near the ceiling. I pointed it out to her with my trembling forefinger and God gave her the grace to see it too. Our bedroom was filled with awe and saturated with glory. We prayed and thanked God for this awesome experience. When prayer becomes a **lifestyle**, experiences like this will become common.

If only we can wait upon the Lord and expect Him to come, He is more than happy to do that anytime, anywhere. When you walk down the stairs at night in your house alone when it is pitch dark, do you expect to see some zombie or ghost? Or, do you expect to see heavenly angels? One of the reasons many people have bad experiences at night, like nightmares, is because they live in fear and do not walk by faith. Prayer is one way to live a life of faith, as it brings Angels down.

Your Prayer Torch

Every believer has a unique calling in their prayer life, a specific area where they are meant to shine the light of God. I like to think of this as your 'prayer torch', it's the particular focus that God has placed in your heart to illuminate through intercession. This revelation is connected to what Jesus said:

> *You are the light of the world. A city set on a hill cannot be hidden. Nor do people light a lamp and put it under a basket, but on a stand, and it gives light to all in the house. In the same way, let your light shine before others, so that they may see your good works and give glory to your Father who is in heaven.*
>
> **(Matthew 5:14-16)**

While this verse speaks to believers being the light of the world in general, it also symbolises the light of prayer that each of us carries. When you pray, you bring illumination to the spiritual realm and shed light on the needs and issues that God has placed on your heart. Just as a lamp brightens a room, your prayers can shine divine light on situations that need change, hope, or healing.

Your prayer torch is not just a symbolic light but a powerful means to drive out darkness, bringing God's truth and presence into specific circumstances. Whether your calling is to pray for the sick, intercede for peace, or stand in the gap for revival, your prayers serve as a beacon that pierces through spiritual darkness.

Examples of Prayer Torches in the Bible

Hannah (1 Samuel 1:10-20) carried her prayer torch with fervent hope for a child, and her specific prayers not only transformed her life but also impacted the future of Israel through her son, Samuel. Nehemiah (Nehemiah 1:4-11) held a torch that lit the way for the restoration of Jerusalem's walls. His dedication to prayer and action brought renewal and hope to a broken city.

Even Anna, the prophetess (Luke 2:36-38), exemplified what it means to hold a prayer torch. For decades, she dedicated her life to praying and fasting for the coming of the Messiah. Her persistence was rewarded when she witnessed the arrival of Jesus, fulfilling the promise she had prayed for so long.

Igniting Your Prayer Torch

What is your prayer torch? What specific burden has God placed on your heart that no one else seems to carry in the same way? Remember, the light of your prayer is not just meant for personal illumination but for impacting the world. Your unique passion is an invitation from God to shine your prayer torch and make a difference. Your prayer light should not be hidden but placed on a stand for all to see and benefit from.

This is not a coincidence; it is a calling. Your unique passion and conviction are clear indicators of where God wants you to direct your prayers. Just as the effectual, fervent prayer of a righteous person has great power, your prayer torch can make a significant difference (James 5:16).

Commit yourself to this calling. Carry your prayer torch boldly, and let it shine through your intercession. Let the world see that light and glorify God because you chose to illuminate it through prayer.

As you close this book, remember that prayer is the

heartbeat of a vibrant, Spirit-filled life. Start with one of these practical methods today, and let it grow into a habit that becomes as natural as breathing. Let your prayer life illuminate the path for others and bring glory to God. The journey begins now. Commit to making prayer your **lifestyle**.

Reflection and Application
Chapter 8: Practical Prayer Ideas

Integrating Prayer with Daily Activities: Consider the different ways you can incorporate prayer into your daily routine, as mentioned in the chapter (e.g., prayer walks, family altar, or prayer music). Which of these practical ideas resonates with you the most?

_____

_____

_____

_____

Establishing a Family Altar: How can you create or enhance a daily or weekly family prayer routine to strengthen spiritual bonds and encourage unity within your home?

_____

_____

_____

Practical Prayer Ideas

Maintaining Focus During Prayer: The chapter explores the use of prayer points and journaling to maintain focus during prayer. What are some ways you can develop and use prayer points or a prayer book to make your prayer sessions more structured and impactful?

_____

_____

_____

_____

_____

_____

_____

_____

_____

_____

_____

_____

Thank You for Reading My Book!

Your support is a blessing to me. I deeply value your feedback and am genuinely interested in hearing your thoughts.

Would you kindly spare a moment to share your insights by leaving a review on Amazon? Your feedback will help me understand your thoughts on the book better.

Thank you immensely for your time and consideration.

Warm regards,
Joe Benjamin

About The Author

Joe Benjamin is a speaker, author, songwriter, entrepreneur, and seasoned business strategist and coach, dedicated to empowering believers for impactful leadership in the marketplace. He believes that the marketplace is the new battleground for spiritual warfare, where God is positioning His people as influential leaders to shape culture and bring transformation.

As the founder of Light Nation, Joe has created a global dynamic platform designed to equip end-time believers to recognise their unique purpose and confidently walk in their divine light.

Joe is married to his beloved wife, Josie, and together they are blessed with two children, Jael Jovanna and Joseph Benjamin III. The couple is renowned for their visionary leadership, innovation, and boldness. Joe and Josie are highly sought-after international conference speakers, inspiring audiences worldwide with their compelling messages and insights.

Visit Joe Benjamin's website here: www.JoeBenjamin.org

Notes

www.ingramcontent.com/pod-product-compliance
Lightning Source LLC
Chambersburg PA
CBHW030304100526
44590CB00012B/511